My
PHILIPS AIRFRYER
EXPANDED
Cookbook

By

Julie Martins

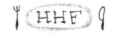

HHF Press
San Francisco

Legal Notice

The information contained in this book is for entertainment purposes only. The content represents the opinion of the author and is based on the author's personal experience and observations. The author does not assume any liability whatsoever for the use of or inability to use any or all information contained in this book, and accepts no responsibility for any loss or damages of any kind that may be incurred by the reader as a result of actions arising from the use of information in this book. Use this information at your own risk.

The author reserves the right to make any changes he or she deems necessary to future versions of the publication to ensure its accuracy.

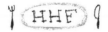

DO YOU LIKE FREE BOOKS?

Every month we release a new book, and we offer it to our current readers first...absolutely free! This helps us get early feedback before launching a book, and lets you stock your shelf full of interesting and valuable books for free!

Some recent titles include:

- The Complete Vegetable Spiralizer Cookbook
- My Lodge Cast Iron Skillet Cookbook
- 101 The New Crepes Cookbook

To receive this month's free book, just go to

http://www.healthyhappyfoodie.org/p3-freebooks

Table Of Contents

Why You Need this Book!   **7**

Why Choose Philips?   **11**

Health Benefits of Air Fried Food   **15**

How to Use your Philips Air Fryer   **19**

Pro Tips to Make Perfect Air Fried Food and Snacks   **25**

Appetizers   **39**
Bacon Cheese Fries   40
Bacon Parmesan Twists   41
Bacon Wrapped Cheese Bombs   43
Crab Rangoon   45
Crispy Egg Plant Caprese Stacks   46
Easy Fried Cheese   47
Fried Eggplant   48
Fried Green Beans   49
Fried Green Olives Stuffed with Blue Cheese   50
Fried Green Tomatoes   51
Fried Pickles   52
Jalapeño Poppers   53
Onion Rings   55

Sides   **57**
Potato Chips   58
Fried Broccoli   59
Fried Zucchini   60
Fried Okra   61
Fried Brussels Sprouts   62
Crispy Cauliflower   63
Fried Bread   64
Nut Butter Crusted Parsnip Fries   65

Vegan / Vegetarian Recipes   **66**
Broccoli Fritters   67
California Fried Walnuts   68

Crispy Buffalo Cauliflower   69
Crispy Salt and Pepper Tofu   70
Fried Artichokes   71
Fried Golden Fuyus   72
Fried Plantains   73
Gobi   74
Parsnip Fries   77
Potato and Pea Patties   78
Pumpkin and Chickpea Fritters   80
Rosemary Sweet Potato Fries   81
Tofu Tater Tots   82
Vegan Egg Nog French Toast   84
Vegan Lemon Cupcakes   85
Zucchini Patties   87

Main Dish Recipes   88

Adobo Crusted Lamb Loin Chops   89
Almond Crusted Chicken Fingers   91
Asian Pork Chops   92
Brown Sugar Brined Turkey   93
Country Fried Steak and Mushroom Gravy   95
Crispy Fried Pork Cutlets   97
Easy Fried Fish Filets   98
Easy Indian Fish Fry   99
Fried Chicken Livers   101
Fried Chicken Sandwich   102
Fried Fish Tacos   103
Fried Haddock   104
Fried Polenta and Mushroom Ragu   105
Fried Ravioli   107
Fried Scallops   108
Fried Squid with Aioli   109
Fried Stuffed Oysters on the Half Shell with Crawfish Stuffing   111
Fried Tortellini   113
Indian Fish Fingers   114
Japanese Style Fried Shrimp   116
Old Bay Crab Cakes   117
Oyster Sandwiches   118
Potato Crusted Salmon   120
Prawn and Mango Spring Rolls   121

Quick Fried Catfish 122
Salmon Croquets 123
Shrimp and Mango Spring Rolls 125
Shrimp Wontons 127
Simple Fried Pork Chops 128
Spicy Southern Fried Chicken 129
Sweet and Spicy Firecracker Chicken 131
Tuna Burgers 132
Tuscan Pork Chops 133

Desserts 135
Apple Fritters 136
Hoddeok 138
Fried Peaches 140
Fried Apple Pie 142
Fried Tequila Shots 144
Mexican Fried Ice Cream 145
Nuégados Guatemaltecos 146

Healthier Snack Options 148
Chilaquiles 149
Fried Asian Cucumber Crisps 150
Wonder Fries 151

Gluten-Free Recipes 153
Beet Burgers 154
Crispy Enoki Mushroom and Onion Fritters 156
Fried Chickpeas 158
Gluten Free Fried Shrimp 159
Pluto Pups 160
Quinoa Cauliflower Patties 161
Salmon Nuggets 163
Shrimp and Egg Pancakes 164
Skinny Carrot Fries 165

BONUS... 166

1

Why You Need this Book!

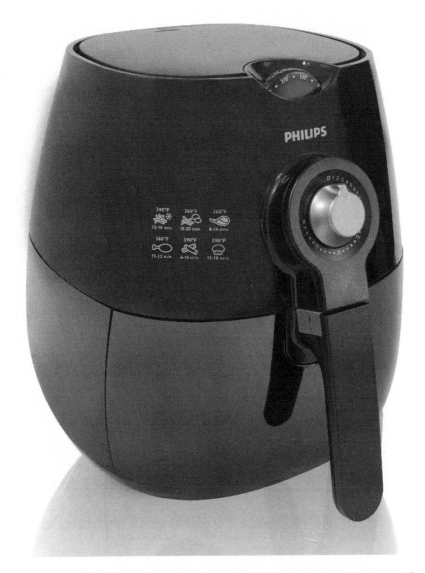

This is The Only Book Written Specifically for The Philips Air Fryer

There are other air fryer books out there, but none are written specifically for the Philips Air Fryer. This book is filled with general air fryer ideas, but it also focuses on some of the great features that are included with the Philips Air Fryer; by the time you are done with this book you will know your appliance better than Philips does. This book is also not some dull copy that reads like an owner's manual, it is meant to be as enjoyable to read as it is to eat the delicious recipes inside.

It Will Unlock the Secrets of the Air Fryer

Air fryers are a relatively new technology which means that most people aren't aware of the secrets that these machines hold. Luckily, a few dedicated people have worked hard to unlock the secrets of air frying in order to pass them onto you. By the end of this book you will know how to perfectly prepare, cook, and serve the most delicious air fried foods that anyone has ever tasted. This book will also tell you how to take care of your air fryer to make sure that is will last for years to come and show you how your air fryer may become your favorite appliance in your entire kitchen.

A Break Down of Safe Operation of Your Philips Air Fryer from Start to Finish

Though using an air fryer is inherently safer that deep frying or pan frying, there are a few safety tips you will want to consider when using your air fryer. This book will break down how to safely prepare your food, operate your machine, remove and handle food, and safely clean and maintain your fryer. You will always feel comfortable and free air-frying your food knowing that you and your family are safer and healthier because of this cooking method.

Learn to Make the Most Delicious Food Possible

Anyone can throw a potato in a fryer and see what happens, but it takes a real pro to know how to deliver tasty and perfectly cooked food every time. This book will take you through the steps to deliver the best air-fried food possible from preparation to the table. Through professional tips to making the most out of your air fryer to comprehensive hand-picked recipes, your final result will be healthier food options that you could never dream of making before. You will become an air-fry master without ever having to take a class.

Learn What Ingredients You Need and How to Store Them

To truly use for air fryer to the fullest you will need to know which ingredients you need to stock in your pantry. You will learn which dry ingredients are used for which recipes and how they should be stored to hold their freshness. You will also learn how to store foods once they have been cooked to ensure the best flavor and texture possible. Every single one of these ingredients can be found at your local grocery store and are all easy to pronounce.

A Comprehensive List of Recipes

Perhaps the most important feature of this book is its comprehensive list of recipes. You will learn how to fry and bake everything from breakfast to dessert and all of our recipes are tried and tested to make sure they are delicious. Recipes are easy to read and follow and, given the nature of the machine, most recipes take less than an hour from preparation to the table. Every single ingredient will be found at your local grocery store and all of them are easy to pronounce.

2

Why Choose Philips?

Exclusive Rapid Air Technology

Philips offers exclusive technology that heats air up to 390 degrees and circulates it evenly around the machine; this ensures that the food is evenly cooked every time. Along with the rapid air technology the machine is also specifically designed to facilitate more even cooking because of its star- shaped bottom. Evenly cooked food gives it that perfectly crisp texture that we are striving for.

Join the Air Frying Revolution

So many people are ditching their old oil fryers and switching to air fryers, that it is actually being called an air frying revolution. It is easy to see why people would want to ditch their old oil fryers now that this new technology is readily available. Air fryers are cleaner, safer, healthier, and easier to use than an oil fryer, not to mention that they take up less space in most instances. If you are the kind of person who likes to be the first on your block to have the newest technology, now is the time to join the air frying revolution before every kitchen around the world is using this outstanding new technology.

Top Reviews Can't Be Wrong

On Amazon the Philips air fryer is rated around 4.5 stars out of 5 and a majority of users—68% to be exact—rated it at 5 out of 5 stars. When it comes to dedicated review websites Philips air fryers win the top rating almost every single time; if you are number one across the board you have to be doing something right. Here are a couple real quotes right from Amazon:

"Well worth the space in my kitchen."

"Buy it!"

"Worth it!"

"As fast as a microwave"

"Tastes similar to an oil fryer."
"The best thing I have EVER purchased"
I could write an entire book of positive reviews for this fryer. There is no doubt that you will want to write a positive review to when you see just what this machine can do.

The Health Benefits

We will dive deeper into the health benefits of using an air fryer later in the book, but for right now it is important to touch on the topic as the health benefits are an important reason to choose a Philips fryer. For most recipes, you will not need to use any oil at all, and for the few that you do the amount of oil is only minuscule percent compared to traditional oil frying.

There are also benefits like more thorough cooking, the option to bake instead of fry, and inherently lower calorie meals. Imagine deliciously crisp fish without the guilt of deep frying or crispy vegetables that retain their nutritional value.

Built to Last

Philips is a well-established company that is always trying to do right by its customers. This product is made to withstand daily use and all of the washable parts are dishwasher safe. Philips has a limited one -year warranty on all of their products which covers any malfunction during proper use. If there may be an issue due to deviation from the proper use, there is always the option to purchase replacement parts on the internet. As long as you use the product the way it is intended to be used will last a long time even with fairly regular use.

3

Health Benefits of Air Fried Food

Uses Little to No Oil

This is perhaps one of the most confusing points about an air fryer, so we will break it down a bit for you.   An air fryer inherently does not need hot oil to cook because it uses hot air to cook the foods.   Air fryers work by rotating super-heated air around the food, essentially cooking foods in their own oils instead of having to coat them with extra oil.   This machine would only need to use oil with specific recipes and in these cases, you can use a low- fat oil like olive oil and only brush the foods.

The fact that it does not use oil in a traditional sense goes far beyond the calorie count, but that is a consideration.   Most fryer manufacturers agree that air frying your food can lower the calorie count of fried foods by up to 80%.   That is a staggering number which would be easy to see on a scale within only a couple of weeks.   Apart from the calorie count, there is another health concern that has been become increasingly important in the past few years.   As we learn more about the world we live in people are becoming increasingly aware of their food allergies and sensitivities – oils and fats being near the top of the list—no need for oil means no need to worry about these concerns when enjoying your perfectly cooked foods.

All the Crispness with Fewer Calories

One of the main draws of fried foods is their crispy outside and soft inside; which up until this point has never been able to be reproduced.   Now you get all of the crispness and flavors of fried foods with only a fraction of the calories.   Not only does this make enjoying fried foods less guilt-full, but it also makes it easier to stomach healthier foods without worrying about losing their health benefits.

Cooked from All Directions to Ensure Thorough Cooking

Any seasoned cook will tell you that there is nothing more frustrating than following all of the rules and still ending up with undercooked food. This can happen in almost any cooking method including oil cooking. Cooking in oil is not an exact science and you could always hit a pocket of oil which is under heated for whatever reason causing uneven cooking of your food.

With air frying, there is never a worry about under cooking, because the method is so precise. Food is cooked at an even temperature from every angle which means that—as long as the basket is not overfilled—all of the food cooks evenly every time. This means that there is no need to worry about any kind of food-borne illness that could come from undercooking.

Safer than Oil Frying

Aside from the calorie count the biggest negative factor of oil frying is that it is downright dangerous. How many times have you half placed, half thrown something into oil and then ran the other direction to avoid the hot oil splatter? If there is even an ounce of moisture on that food you are looking at a 4th of July display of hot oil all over the kitchen—and probably your skin.

If there is one concern more important than burning your skin it may be burning your whole house down. The lack of oil frying means no oil to start kitchen fires which could eventually lead to a house fire. This may not be a selling point to buying an air fryer but it is definitely a big benefit.

Food Keeps its Nutrients

One of the biggest health benefits besides fewer calories is that food actually keeps its nutrients. In almost any cooking method food—especially vegetables—loses any nutrients it may have through the cooking process. Since air frying cooks by sealing the natural juices in instead of cooking them out it naturally seals in all of the nutrients as well making air frying one of the healthiest ways ever to cook vegetables.

No Transfats or Other Potentially Harmful Food Additives

When you are not cooking with oil you are not cooking with any transfats either. These fatty oils have been condemned in recent years for their harmful effects on the body. The fact that you only need hot air to cook foods in this machine means that you don't need to add anything at all in order to produce delicious meals without harmful byproducts.

4

How to Use your Philips Air Fryer

This chapter will explain how to use your air fryer to its maximum potential. It will not offer any recipes, but it will tell you the basics of frying, baking, cleaning, and more. Before you even put anything in your fryer there are a few things you are going to want to do. First of all, you want to make sure that your fryer is on a flat and stable surface, even though it doesn't use oil it can still get very hot and you don't want it falling on you or any kid or pet that may be around your feet at the time. It is equally important that you place your fryer on a burn resistant surface for obvious reasons. Make sure that the fryer is plugged in and attach the basket to the device. From there, you are ready to cook some of the most delicious healthy food you have ever had.

How to Fry

You wouldn't have bought an air fryer if you weren't looking to air fry food, so this is a pretty good place to start. Start by placing your food in the basket, be careful not to overfill it as it could hurt the machine and cause uneven cooking. Next, you can set your cook time and temperature manually using the digital display. If you are frying using a cold basket add 3 minutes onto your cook time, if you have the time you can preheat the basket by setting the appropriate temperature and setting the time to 4 minutes. When it is ready, the "heating up" light will turn off; it is not uncommon for the light to turn on and off during cooking, this indicates that the heating element is turning on and off to maintain the set temperature.

For some foods you will want to toss the ingredient while cooking. Simply pull the basket out (the machine will pause) toss the ingredients, then return the basket. As long as you follow these simple steps you will end up with perfectly air fried food that will be a hit with the whole family. When the cook time has been reached the machine will automatically shut down to avoid overcooking. Pull the pan out and place it on a heat- resistant surface; be careful when tipping the pan or removing food as the natural oils from the food will collect at the bottom of the pan. As long as you follow these simple step you should come out with perfectly air fried food every time.

How to Bake

You probably didn't buy an air fryer to bake cupcakes, but the idea is intriguing now that you know you can. The cooking procedure is pretty much the same as frying with a few minor adjustments. The biggest difference is that you are going to want to bake your foods inside of a baking tin which you place in the basket. As with any baking the temperature changes depending on what you are baking, but here is a short list of ballpark baking ranges.

CAKE: 320 DEGREES FOR 20 – 25 MINUTES
QUICHE: 360 DEGREES FOR 20 – 22 MINUTES
MUFFINS: 390 DEGREES FOR 15-18 MINUTES

Timer and Temperature Control

Philips embraces the technological world we live in with a digital timer and temperature control. Using the interface could not be any simpler with only four buttons on the face. First, you turn it on, then select the time or temperature (one button toggles both), scroll to the desired time and temperature, and let it go. The timer will beep to inform you when it is done and the machine will automatically shut off to prevent injury, damage, or burnt food.

Important Basket Considerations

The basket is not extremely complicated, but as one of the most important parts of the machine it deserves a bit of attention. Make sure to never over fill the basket or put anything in the basket that is not supposed to be there. Not only could you ruin your dinner, but you could also ruin an integral part of your machine. Also, never touch the basket anywhere other than the handle as the basket can get hot enough to burn your skin.

When your food is done cooking you will remove the pan and the basket from the machine and place the pan on a heat safe surface. To remove the basket from the pan, slide the button guard on the basket handle forward and press the button to release the basket from the pan. From there, you can toss your ingredients or empty them onto a plate. Once you return the basket to the pan you will hear it click back into place.

If you choose to use a utensil to remove your food instead of pouring it out, make sure to use a utensil that is not metal or abrasive in any way as it could damage the non-stick coating of the basket.

How to Clean and Maintain your Air Fryer

Your air fryer should be clean after every use; make sure that it has sufficiently cooled before you take it apart to clean it. The outside of the fryer, including the top and screen, can be wiped down with a moist cloth as it should not be getting very dirty. You can clean the pan and basket just like any dishes with warm water and soap; again make sure that you are using a sponge that will not damage the non-stick surface of the basket. If manual labor is not your cup of tea, the basket and the pan are also dishwasher safe. To clean the inside of the machine, use a damp cloth or sponge, be careful not to get the inside of the machine too wet. If there is any food debris on the heating element it can be cleaned using a cleaning brush. As long as you clean your machine thoroughly and often it should continue to produce great tasting food for quite a long time.

5

Pro Tips to Make Perfect Air Fried Food and Snacks

Preparation is King

The key to perfectly air fried food is perfectly preparing the food before you cook it. Without proper preparation, your food will come out less than satisfactory or even inedible. Here are a few suggestions for preparation of common air fried foods.

FRIES/CHIPS

Potato dishes are probably the only dishes you will ever need to use oil with. A tablespoon of olive oil in a full basket will help to make sure that your fries are crisp on the outside and soft on the inside. I like to mix together a 50/50 mix of sea salt and fresh ground pepper to season my fries before I cook them. If you are cooking regular potatoes it is advised that you cut them up for better cooking, but if you do want to cook whole potatoes make sure that they are smaller and don't over fill the basket.

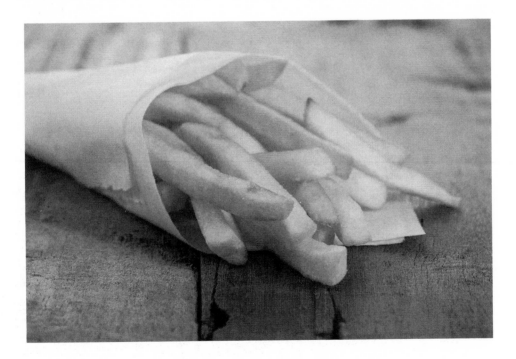

STEAK AND OTHER MEAT CUTS

Meats are fairly easy to prepare; the most important part of meat preparation is making sure that you give yourself enough time. When you are simply seasoning a cut there is not a lot of preparation time that goes into it. All you need to do is lightly coat both sides in seasoning shortly before cooking. If you are having trouble evenly coating your cuts, pat them down with a wet cloth to help the seasoning to stick.

Marinating your cuts is an entirely different venture that takes a little more time. Depending on the cut and the marinade it could take up to 24 hours to prepare the perfect meal. Most often it will take a minimum of 4 hours to marinate your cuts in order for them to absorb all of the juices of the marinade. The great thing about air frying a marinated cut of meat is that it seals all of the marinade inside instead of cooking it out.

SHRIMP

There may not seem like a lot of ways to prepare shrimp, but it is surprising how much can be done with the most popular edible crustacean. For the most, part you are going to want to toss your shrimp not matter how you are coating it. I like to use a large plastic storage container with a lid to toss anything I am cooking; they do the job, and are easily washable. If you are using a dry seasoning, you may want to lightly toss your shrimp in water or oil to ensure an even coating that sticks to the shrimp.

It is not extremely common to marinate shrimp, so we will skip paste that, but it is common to bread your shrimp before frying. For this method, you will want white flour, egg, and whatever you have chosen as your breading. Make sure your shrimp is completely thawed before breading. Coat the shrimp in flour, then dip it in a bowl of beaten egg, then coat it in your breading before transferring to the basket.

BAKED GOODS

There is not a lot to say about the preparation of baked goods, other than to make sure that you follow the baking instructions carefully. If you have ever cooked a cake without eggs you know what I mean, and if you haven't I would not suggest trying it. One note I would add is to make sure that you use a pan in the basket and make sure that you coat the pan with cooking spray before you add your ingredients.

CHICKEN

If only preparing chicken was half as fun as eating it. For the most part preparing chicken is much like preparing any other protein. If you are looking to prepare non-breaded chicken, you can season it by tossing it in dry seasoning. Make sure to pat down the chicken with a wet cloth to get an even coating of seasoning.

Chicken can also be marinated in any number of marinades from classic buffalo sauce to a marinade of your own concoction. Chicken absorbs marinades fairly well so it should only take 4 to 6 hours to perfectly marinade your chicken.

It would be a travesty to not talk about preparing breaded chicken; considering the fact that breaded chicken almost universally goes by the name of fried chicken. Whether you are cooking breaded chicken strips or bone-in chicken breasts the method is going to be the same. Coat your chicken in flour, then dip it in a bowl of beaten egg, lastly coat it in whatever breading you have chosen before placing it in your basket.

FISH

Preparing fish is much like preparing any other protein with a few slight changes. Seasoning fish is a little more difficult due to its delicate nature, tossing it will almost surely break it up into pieces. Instead keep an old pepper shaker around to keep your fish seasoning in. You should never have to wet your fish, again due to its nature.

Breading fish is much like breading any other protein, you just need to be more delicate when you do it. Coat the filet in flour, then dip it in a bowl of beaten egg before coating it in your choice of breading. Again, be careful in every step leading up to placing the fish in the basket as fish can be delicate and fall apart easily.

Timing is Everything

Preparing your food is important, but all the preparation in the world will not make up for over or under cooking. It is important to always make sure that you are cooking your foods according to their proper cook times. Every item is different, but here is a breakdown of the ranges of temperature and time for each of the most common foods.

- Potatoes: Potatoes very because of the many sizes of different potato configurations. Most potatoes cook between 360 and 390 degrees and 10 to 20 minutes.
- Steak: For a perfectly cooked steak you are looking at 8-12 minutes at 360 degrees.
- Chicken Wings: Chicken wings will take about 18 – 22 minutes to cook at 360 degrees.

- Pork/Lamb: These cuts will take about 10 – 14 minutes at 360 degrees.
- Premade Frozen Snacks: Most premade frozen snacks usually take 6 – 10 minutes at 390 degrees.
- Baking: It is impossible to generalize baking since each dish requires its own cook time, for the most part following the traditional baking guidelines should work for your air fryer.

Match the Correct Seasoning to the Correct Foods

Matching the correct seasoning to the correct dish is not rocket science, but you can't just toss any old seasoning on any dish and expect it to taste good.   The following are a few recommendations for some of the most common foods.

- Fries/Chips: Sea salt, kosher salt, pepper, rosemary, Cajun spice, garlic salt, parsley, paprika, and old bay seasoning.
- Steaks: Spice blends made specifically for steak, butter, salt, and pepper.
- There are not a lot of recommended spices for steak because steaks are seen as flavorful enough when cooked correctly.
- Pork: Rosemary, sage, parsley, marjoram, thyme, caraway seeds, spice mixes made for poultry, lemon pepper, spice mixes made specifically for pork.
- Lamb: Rosemary, fennel, oregano, cumin, vadouvan, harissa, sumac
- Chicken: Spice mixes made specifically for poultry, tarragon, thyme, lemon grass, basil, sage, rosemary, parsley, marjoram, salt, and pepper.
- Chicken is awesome because pretty much anything can be used to enhance the flavor of the chicken.

- Fish/Shellfish: Tarragon, citrus zest, lemon thyme, dill, lemon grass, pepper, Cajun seasoning, basil, fennel seed, parsley, basil, mustard seed, and spice mixes made specifically for fish.
- Fish is a lot like chicken in the fact that almost everything goes with it; the difference is that spicing fish is usually to take the edge off the taste, not to enhance its natural flavor.
- Vegetables: Salt, pepper, citrus zest, and Cajun spice. There is not a lot to be done with vegetables, and in most cases, you won't need to, but it is nice to have a little change every once in a while.

Always Use High- Quality Ingredients

This one may seem like a no-brainer to some, but many people still try to cut corners when it comes to their food from the quality of their cuts to the freshness of their spices. If you are not using the freshest and highest quality of ingredients when you are preparing and cooking your food it could come out sub-par. A novice—or bull headed—cook may try to blame the air fryer, but 9 times out of 10 it is due to user error.

Never Leave Foods While they are Cooking

You should never leave your air fryer alone for too long while you are cooking, because you never know what could happen. These machines are relatively safe, but it is always better to be safe than sorry with any appliance. Beyond that, there are very few foods that do not need to be shifted in some way during cooking. Always make sure to toss, shake, or turn your foods during cooking to ensure an even cooking and no burning which could eventually lead to issues.

Do NOT Overfill Your Machine

It may seem like a great idea to get everything done at once, or maybe you are just really hungry, but overfilling the machine can lead to disaster. The best case scenario is that your food will not cook evenly which will leave you even worse off than you were before you started cooking. Other alternatives include breaking your machine or even starting a fire if the basket is full enough.

Always add the recommended amount of food and remember that an air fryer cooks rather fast so it is not a big deal to have to cook multiple batches.

Always Put Your Food in Dry

Apart from the health issues, the biggest complaints about frying traditional foods is the smell and the smoke involved in the cooking process. For the most part, these inconveniences are completely avoided when cooking with an air fryer, unless your food is overly saturated. To prevent thick white smoke and a smell from coming from your fryer make sure that that your food is relatively dry. It does not need to be bone dry since you could have a marinade or a rather juicy cut of meat, but it should not be dripping. In order to avoid this issue, pat your food down with a dry paper towel before placing it in the basket. If there is a large amount of smoke coming from your fryer, don't freak out. Simply stop your timer, dry off the foods, and restart at the stopped time. This should stop the issue and prevent any further issues, if the problem continues you may have to wait it out a few minutes; remember that it won't hurt you or the machine, it is just a little unpleasant.

Don't be Afraid to Experiment

If you take one thing away from this chapter, or this entire book it should be that you should never be afraid to experiment when cooking. Whether it is trying a new spice on a dish or changing the heat or the cooking time; the worst that can happen is that you may end up having to order a pizza. No great cook became a great cook by following a recipe book and the sandwich had to be invented by someone. Go out there and make a difference in the world by experimenting with your food; maybe someday you will write a recipe book of your own.

Adapting Your Favorite Recipes

If you have some favorite recipes that are not covered in this book, don't worry. Most recipes can be adapted by simply keeping the cooking temperature the same, but changing the time as the oil-less fryer will cook for food much faster than a traditional oven.

How to Store Your Air Fried Foods?

When it comes to fried food, storage can be a pain in the you-know-what. You want to make sure that your fried food stays crispy and keeps all of its delicious flavors without going bad by being left out. A lot depends on the kind of foods that you are cooking, but there are a few storage options that allow you to have your literal and metaphorical cake and eat it too.

Always Set Prepared Foods on a Cooling Rack

Even though you are not frying with oil you are still frying food which means that the outside of your food is going to be crispy and you are going to want to keep it that way. When you place fried foods on a flat surface, residual heat builds up underneath the foods and releases steam which will, in turn, make your foods soggy. By setting fried foods on a cooling rack it allows that heat to escape which will keep your foods crispier longer. This is a perfect way to store fried foods if you are cooking multiple servings for supper or making a large batch that will be served in 4 hours or less.

The Oven Method

If you are looking to keep a large amount of food warm and ready to serve the oven method may be the perfect storage option for you. This is one of my favorite ways to keep fried foods for short periods of time. While you are frying your foods preheat your oven; the temperature really depends on how hot you want the food to be served, but it should never exceed 300 degrees otherwise you are going to continue to cook your food and it will end up being too dry.

Line a baking sheet with a thick layer of paper towels; it will absorb excess grease without posing a fire risk. Add foods to the sheet as they come out of the fryer and keep them in the oven until they are ready to serve. It is not an overnight storage solution but it can keep foods perfectly warm and crisp for a few hours.

Let Them Cool Before Storing

If you absolutely must store your foods in a refrigerator you have to at least let them fully cool before storing them. Use the cooling rack method to let the all of the excess heat evaporate and make sure that the food is completely cool (sometimes up to 2 hours) before placing your food in plastic storage containers. You can also pierce small holes in the top of the storage containers to allow anymore condensation to release. Food stored in storage containers can last up to a week or more; when you are ready to eat it you can always pop it in the air fryer for a few minutes to heat it back up or just pop it in the microwave. It may not have its right out of the fryer crispness, but it should maintain a little crispness and all of the flavor.

Store Baked Goods in Paper or Plastic Wrap

This method of storage has been utilized for decades, the surprising thing here is that you can create baked goods with your air fryer. Whether you are cooking a traditional cake, or even making donuts, they can be stored for long periods of time in brown paper or plastic wrap in order to maintain their freshness for a longer period of time.

Freeze them in Storage Bags

There may be a reoccurring theme here, but you should let your food cool completely before freezing it to avoid condensation which will render your food soggy no matter what you do. Once your food is properly cooled you can place it in a freezer bag and push out as much air as possible before freezing it. When you are ready to serve your food let it thaw and then toss it in the fryer or a microwave to reheat it. It will not have its same crispness, but it will retain a little crispness and all of the flavor.

Wrap it in Foil

If you absolutely need to store food without an adequate cooling time the best way to store it is by wrapping it in tin foil. The foil will draw some of the heat out to keep it from creating condensation and making the food soggy. Foil works to keep the food ready to serve in minutes or days which makes it one of the best options for fried food period.

6

Appetizers

Bacon Cheese Fries

Servings: 8 | Prep Time: 25 Minutes | Cook Time: 5 Minutes

You may have seen this recipe at your favorite casual dining restaurant but now you can enjoy it in the comfort of your own home. The best part is that this is a super simple recipe that does not take a lot of actual engagement to complete.

Ingredients:

1 package (32-ounce) frozen french fried potatoes

1 cup shredded cheddar cheese

1/2 cup thinly sliced green onions

1/4 cup diced Jalapeños

1/4 cup crumbled cooked bacon

Instructions:

1. Cook fries per instructions on bag.

2. Place in a pan and sprinkle over cheese, bacon, green onions, and jalapeños.

3. Place in the basket and cook in your Philips at 400 degrees for 5 minutes or until the cheese has melted.

Nutritional Info: Calories: 153, Sodium: 151 mg, Dietary Fiber: 3.2 g, Total Fat: 5.8 g, Total Carbs: 19.3 g, Protein: 6.5 g.

Bacon Parmesan Twists

Servings: 3 | Prep Time: 25 Minutes | Cook Time: 20 Minutes

These take a fair amount of work, but the work is well worth the final result. They are unlike anything else you will ever see or taste, and a guaranteed crowd pleaser.

Ingredients:

1 x 14 ounce puff pastry sheet

Plain flour, for dusting, if not using parchment to roll your pastry

1 tablespoon Dijon mustard

1/4 cup freshly grated parmesan

8-9 slices good-quality streaky bacon

1 egg

Instructions:

1. Lay one piece of bacon out and roll out your pastry until it is the same height as your bacon.

2. Spread your mustard evenly over the pastry leaving about 1/4 of an inch clear around the edges.

3. Sprinkle the parmesan evenly over the mustard.

4. Place bacon strips evenly over the cheese leaving enough room between each strip to cut.

5. Cut between each slice; a pizza cutter makes this job easier.

6. Grab the top of your first slice and carefully twist it 4 to 5 times or until the bacon and pastry are totally wrapped around each other; repeat this for each individual stick.

7. Place the twists flat on a pan or plate and refrigerate them for 20 minutes.

8.   After 20 minutes, remove the twists and brush them with your beaten egg.

9.   Bake in your Philips air fryer at 400 degrees for 20 minutes.

Nutritional Info: Calories: 329, Sodium: 1337 mg, Dietary Fiber: 0 g, Total Fat: 24.8 g, Total Carbs: 1.4 g, Protein: 23.9 g.

Bacon Wrapped Cheese Bombs

Servings: 10 | Prep Time: 10 Minutes | Cook Time: 10 Minutes

Just the name of this appetizer makes your mouth start watering. The recipe is pretty straight forward and does not take a lot of ingredients. The only thing you need to worry about is making enough to keep the family happy.

Ingredients:

5 slices of bacon, cut in half

6 ounces brick mozzarella cheese

1 can biscuits

3 tablespoons butter

2 garlic cloves

Toothpicks

Instructions:

1. Cut your cheese into 1 inch by 1 inch squares.

2. Melt your butter and mince the garlic, then combine.

3. Open your biscuits and flatten them, make sure they are not too thin or your cheese will burst through the biscuit wall.

4. Brush the biscuit with your butter mix, flip it, and place your cheese cube in the center.

5. Close the biscuit around the cheese cube and roll it in your hands a few times.

6. Repeat steps 3 and 4 with each biscuit until you have used all of your biscuits.

7. Wrap each biscuit in a half slice of bacon and secure it with a tooth pick.

8. Cook in your Philips air fryer for 8-10 minutes at 360 degrees shaking half way through.

Nutritional Info: Calories: 142, Sodium: 377 mg, Dietary Fiber: 0 g, Total Fat: 10.9 g, Total Carbs: 2.3 g, Protein: 8.6 g.

Crab Rangoon

Servings: 4 | Prep Time: 5 Minutes | Cook Time: 10 Minutes

Crab rangoons are a Chinese restaurant favorite due to their taste and texture. Now you can be the hero at your next house party, or on a random weeknight with how easy these are to make.

Ingredients:

5 ounces picked backfin crabmeat

4 ounces cream cheese, room temperature

1 scallion, thinly sliced

1 clove garlic, finely chopped

1 teaspoon worcestershire sauce

1/2 tablespoon toasted sesame oil

Sea salt and freshly ground black pepper

12 wonton wrappers

Instructions:

1. Mix together all ingredients, but salt, pepper, and wrappers.
2. Add salt and pepper to taste and mix for another minute.
3. Roll out each of your wonton wrappers.
4. Drop in 1/2 teaspoon of crab mix in each wrapper.
5. Fold each wonton and place in the basket.
6. Cook at 400 degrees in your Philips air fryer for 10 minutes.

Nutritional Info: Calories: 431, Sodium: 946 mg, Dietary Fiber: 2 g, Total Fat: 13.2 g, Total Carbs: 62.4 g, Protein: 14.4 g.

Crispy Egg Plant Caprese Stacks

Servings: 2 | Prep Time: 10 Minutes | Cook Time: 10 Minutes

If you are looking to make a statement, look no further than this dish. It is just as much a work of art as it is an appetizer. It doesn't hurt that these flavors combined create a succulent starter.

Ingredients:

2 ripe tomatoes

1 (8-ounce) ball fresh mozzarella

6-8 leaves fresh basil

1/2 cup panko breadcrumbs

6 slices eggplant

1/4 cup flour

1 egg

Instructions:

1. Cut eggplant, tomatoes, and mozzarella each into 1/4-inch-thick pieces.

2. Rinse the basil and pat it dry.

3. In 3 separate bowls pour flour, panko, and beat an egg.

4. Toss eggplant in flour, dip in egg, then toss in panko.

5. Cook in your Philips at 320 degrees for 10 minutes, flipping once.

6. Stack eggplant, tomato, mozzarella, and basil and serve.

Nutritional Info: Calories: 885, Sodium: 951 mg, Dietary Fiber: 51.6 g, Total Fat: 26.8 g, Total Carbs: 121.2 g, Protein: 55.0 g.

Easy Fried Cheese

Servings: 12 | Prep Time: 7 Minutes | Cook Time: 10 Minutes

There is just something special about fried cheese, and this recipe is extra special. With this recipe, you get all of the crunch with a little bit of a kick at the end. Though there are a ton of fried cheese recipes out there, this is the only one you will ever need.

Ingredients:

1 1/2 pounds firm cheese, cut into sticks about one inch wide (1 x 1 x 2 1/2) and chilled

3 cups flour for coating the cheese

1 teaspoon ancho chili powder

3 large eggs

1 teaspoon water

4 cups crushed corn flakes

Instructions:

1. Start by beating your eggs in a shallow bowl, then mix in the water.

2. In another bowl, mix together your flour and chili powder; put the corn flakes in a third bowl.

3. Roll your cheese sticks in the flour mix, dip them in the egg mix, and finally coat them in the corn flakes.

4. Cook in your Philips air fryer for 8-10 minutes at 360 degrees shaking half way through.

Nutritional Info: Calories: 395.7, Sodium: 539 mg, Dietary Fiber: 1.3 g, Total Fat: 20.3 g, Total Carbs: 33.1 g, Protein: 19.5 g.

Fried Eggplant

Servings: 4 | Prep Time: 10 Minutes | Cook Time: 10 Minutes

Eggplant is actually a brilliant food to fry because it is pretty bland by itself. This recipe allows eggplant to keep all of its key nutrients while making it satisfying in both taste and texture.

Ingredients:

1 medium eggplant

1 egg

1/4 cup milk

1 cup Italian bread crumbs

1/2 cup parmesan cheese

Salt and pepper to taste

Instructions:

1. Beat the egg in a shallow bowl and mix in milk.
2. In another bowl, mix together bread crumbs, parmesan, salt, and pepper.
3. Cut eggplant into 1/2-inch-thick slices.
4. Dip in egg mix, then toss in breadcrumbs until evenly coated.
5. Cook in your Philips air fryer at 350 degrees for 10 minutes, flipping halfway through.

Nutritional Info: Calories: 174, Sodium: 510 mg, Dietary Fiber: 5 g, Total Fat: 3.9 g, Total Carbs: 27.7 g, Protein: 8.2 g.

Fried Green Beans

Servings: 4 | Prep Time: 5 Minutes | Cook Time: 5 Minutes

Fried green beans are an appetizer option on restaurant menus across America, and now they can be on your home menu as well. They are super simple and super-fast to make which means you can appease the masses quickly when they are so hungry they are ready to mutiny.

Ingredients:

2 dozen green beans

1/2 cup flour

1/2 cup milk

1 cup panko

1/2 tablespoon garlic powder

1/2 tablespoon oregano

Instructions:

1. Combine panko, garlic, and oregano in a bowl.
2. Pour flour into a separate bowl, and milk into a third bowl.
3. Roll each bean in flour, then milk, and finally the panko mix.
4. Repeat step 3 so each bean is double breaded.
5. Cook in your Philips at 350 degrees for 5 minutes, shaking.

Nutritional Info: Calories: 286, Sodium: 232 mg, Dietary Fiber: 13.2 g, Total Fat: 2.7 g, Total Carbs: 57.5 g, Protein: 12.5 g.

Fried Green Olives Stuffed with Blue Cheese

Servings: 6 | Prep Time: 10 Minutes | Cook Time: 10 Minutes

These olives are a delicious appetizer for any event. They can be prepared ahead of time making them the perfect party snack because they can be cooked and served in 10 minutes. They are best when served hot while the cheese is still melted.

Ingredients:

1 ounce mild blue cheese

24 pitted spanish olives

All-purpose flour

1 large egg, beaten to blend

1/2 cup fine dry breadcrumbs

Instructions:

1. Drain olives and pat them down with a paper towel.
2. Roll a small amount of blue cheese into a cylinder shape and stuff it into the center of the olive; repeat for all olives.
3. If you are short on time steps 1 and 2 can be done a day before and stored in a covered dish in the fridge.
4. Place the flour, egg, and bread crumbs in 3 separate bowls.
5. Roll each olive in flour, dip it in egg, and then roll it in bread crumbs until evenly coated.
6. Using your Philips air fryer, cook at 320 for 10 minutes, tossing a few times during cooking.

Nutritional Info: Calories: 87, Sodium: 407 mg, Dietary Fiber: 1.1 g, Total Fat: 4.6 g, Total Carbs: 8.1 g, Protein: 3.6 g.

Fried Green Tomatoes

Servings: 4 | Prep Time: 15 Minutes | Cook Time: 10 Minutes

Fried green tomatoes are simple, yet almost addictive they are so good. This would be an awesome appetizer for a summer party or a movie night while screening the movie of the same name.

Ingredients:

4 medium green tomatoes

1 teaspoon salt

1/8 teaspoon lemon pepper seasoning

3/4 cups cornmeal

2 tablespoons flour

Instructions:

1. Cut tomatoes into thick slices discarding both ends.
2. Mix together the salt and lemon pepper; and sprinkle both sides of each slice.
3. Let the slices stand for 10 minutes.
4. Mix the flour and cornmeal together until even.
5. Coat each slice in the cornmeal mixture.
6. Cook at 350 degrees in your Philips air fryer for 10 minutes, flipping halfway through.

Nutritional Info: Calories: 119, Sodium: 595 mg, Dietary Fiber: 3.3 g, Total Fat: 1.1 g, Total Carbs: 25.4 g, Protein: 3.4 g.

Fried Pickles

Servings: 16 | Prep Time: 5 Minutes | Cook Time: 10 Minutes

This may be the easiest recipe in this book and it has a high yield making it a great party recipe. Guests will be surprised at how delicious these fried pickles are and you will feel happy knowing that you are serving an appetizer that is not dripping with fat.

Ingredients:

1 quart whole dill pickles

1 cup buttermilk

2 cups plain cornmeal

1 tablespoon sea salt

Instructions:

1. Remove the pickles from the jar and pat them down with a paper towel.

2. Quarter the pickles lengthwise.

3. Put the buttermilk in one bowl and mix together the cornmeal and salt in a separate bowl.

4. Dip each pickle in the butter milk, then roll it in the cornmeal mix until completely covered.

5. Using your Philips, lay your pickles in a single layer in the basket and cook for 10 minutes at 320 degrees, tossing the food halfway through.

Nutritional Info: Calories: 66, Sodium: 841 mg, Dietary Fiber: 1.6 g, Total Fat: 0.8 g, Total Carbs: 13.3 g, Protein: 1.9 g.

Jalapeño Poppers

Servings: 4 | Prep Time: 10 Minutes | Cook Time: 10 Minutes

Jalapeño poppers may be the quintessential appetizer. This simple recipe will be the hit at any party or just as a special treat for the family. The best part is that it is easy and quick to make and just as quick to cook.

Ingredients:

12-18 whole fresh jalapeño

1 cup nonfat refried beans

1 cup shredded Monterey Jack or extra-sharp cheddar cheese

1 scallion, sliced

1 teaspoon salt, divided

1/4 cup all-purpose flour

2 large eggs

1/2 cup fine cornmeal

Olive oil or canola oil cooking spray

Instructions:

1. Start by slicing each jalapeño lengthwise on one side. Place the jalapeños side by side in a microwave safe bowl and microwave them until they are slightly soft; usually around 5 minutes.

2. While your jalapeños cook; mix refried beans, scallions, 1/2 teaspoon salt, and cheese in a bowl.

3. Once your jalapeños are softened you can scoop out the seeds and add one tablespoon of your refried bean mixture (It can be a little less if the pepper is smaller.) Press the jalapeño closed around the filling.

4. Beat your eggs in a small bowl and place your flour in a separate bowl. In a third bowl mix your cornmeal and the remaining salt in a third bowl.

5. Roll each pepper in the flour, then dip it in the egg, and finally roll it in the cornmeal making sure to coat the entire pepper.

6. Place the peppers on a flat surface and coat them with a cooking spray; olive oil cooking spray is suggested.

7. Cook in your Philips air fryer at 400 degrees for 5 minutes, turn each pepper, and then cook for another 5 minutes; serve hot.

Nutritional Info: Calories: 244, Sodium: 800 mg, Dietary Fiber: 2.4 g, Total Fat: 12.5 g, Total Carbs: 20.7 g, Protein: 12.8 g.

Onion Rings

Servings: 4 | Prep Time: 10 Minutes | Cook Time: 10 Minutes

There is no need to pay extravagant restaurant prices for delicious onion rings when you can make delicious onion rings right in your kitchen. The only thing easier than making these onion rings is going to be eating them. Though it will take a few batches to fill the whole recipe it still won't take too long and they are totally worth it.

Ingredients:

1 large spanish onion

1/2 cup buttermilk

2 eggs, lightly beaten

3/4 cups unbleached all-purpose flour

3/4 cups panko bread crumbs

1/2 teaspoon baking powder

1/2 teaspoon Cayenne pepper, to taste

Salt

Instructions:

1. Start by cutting your onion into 1/2 thick rings and separate. Smaller pieces can be discarded or saved for other recipes.

2. Beat the eggs in a large bowl and mix in the buttermilk, then set it aside.

3. In another bowl combine flour, pepper, bread crumbs, and baking powder.

4. Use a large spoon to dip a whole ring in the buttermilk, then pull it through the flour mix on both sides to completely coat the ring.

5.   Cook about 8 rings at a time in your Philips air fryer for 8-10 minutes at 360 degrees shaking half way through.

Nutritional Info: Calories: 225, Sodium: 253 mg, Dietary Fiber: 2.4 g, Total Fat: 3.8 g, Total Carbs: 38.0 g, Protein: 19.3 g.

7

Sides

Potato Chips

Servings: 3 per large potato | Prep Time: 20 Minutes | Cook Time: 15 Minutes

It would be almost criminal not to use an air fryer to make potato chips. These chips are delicious and a much healthier option than deep frying at home or even buying them from the store. Cooking these chips is also a great introductory recipe to get to know your air fryer.

Ingredients:

Russet potatoes

Salt

Pepper

1/2 tablespoon olive oil

Instructions:

1. Start by washing and peeling your potatoes.
2. Adjust a slicer to the thinnest slice possible and slice your potatoes lengthwise. You can cut them manually but it is a guarantee that your chips will be thicker and take longer to cook.
3. Place your slices into a bowl of water and let them soak for about 10 minutes.
4. After 10 minutes rinse your slices and pat them dry with a paper towel.
5. Toss your chips in the olive oil, salt, and pepper.
6. Air-fry using your Philips at 360 degrees for 15 minutes, shaking a few times during cooking.

Nutritional Info: Calories: 167, Sodium: 13 mg, Dietary Fiber: 5.1 g, Total Fat: 2.5 g, Total Carbs: 33.5 g, Protein: 3.6 g.

Fried Broccoli

Servings: 4 | Prep Time: 5 Minutes | Cook Time: 10 Minutes

With a recipe like this you will never have to beg your kids to eat their broccoli again. This recipe curbs the sometimes pungent taste of broccoli while making it crispy on the outside and soft on the inside.

Ingredients:

4 cups of frozen broccoli florets

1 large egg

1/2 cup of milk

1 1/2 cups of self-rising flour

1/2 teaspoon of sea salt

1/4 teaspoon of freshly ground black pepper

1/4 to 1/2 teaspoon of Cajun seasoning

Instructions:

1. In a shallow bowl beat your eggs, then mix in your milk and a half cup of flour.

2. In a separate bowl mix together the remaining flour, Cajun seasoning, salt, and pepper.

3. Dip the broccoli florets in the egg mix, then toss it flour mix.

4. Cook in your Philips air fryer at 320 degrees for 10 minutes, tossing halfway through.

Nutritional Info: Calories: 235, Sodium: 300 mg, Dietary Fiber: 3.7 g, Total Fat: 2.6 g, Total Carbs: 43.5 g, Protein: 10.0 g.

Fried Zucchini

Servings: 4 | Prep Time: 10 Minutes | Cook Time: 10 Minutes

Zucchini is not exactly thought of as the most delicious vegetable to most people, but this recipe will probably be winning it some fans. It is easy to prep, cooks quickly, and a great side to pair with many meals.

Ingredients:

3 large zucchini

1/2 cup all-purpose flour

1 1/2 cups panko bread crumbs

1/4 cup finely grated Parmesan

2 tablespoons finely chopped fresh parsley leaves

1/2 teaspoon red pepper flakes

Salt and freshly ground black pepper

3 eggs

1/4 cup water

Instructions:

1. Pour flour into a shallow bowl

2. In another shallow bowl combine panko, parsley, parmesan, red pepper flakes, salt, and pepper and mix well.

3. In a third bowl lightly beat the eggs, then mix in water.

4. Slice the zucchini into thin slices, then coat in flour.

5. Dip each slice into egg, then toss in panko mix until evenly covered.

6. Cook at 320 degrees in your Philips for 10 minutes, tossing half way through.

Nutritional Info: Calories: 312, Sodium: 392 mg, Dietary Fiber: 5.0 g, Total Fat: 6.6 g, Total Carbs: 49.8 g, Protein: 15.0 g.

Fried Okra

Servings: 4 | Prep Time: 10 Minutes | Cook Time: 10 Minutes

There are few things more southern than fried okra, and this recipe keeps all of that southern taste without those southern calories. This is a great side to serve with some Louisiana meat dishes.

Ingredients:

1 cup yellow cornmeal

1/4 cup all-purpose flour

2 teaspoons coarse salt

1/2 teaspoon cayenne pepper

1/4 teaspoon freshly ground pepper

3 large egg whites

3 teaspoons water

1 pound okra

Instructions:

1. Trim okra and slice diagonally into 1/2 inch pieces.
2. Mix flour, cayenne pepper, cornmeal, salt, and pepper into a shallow bowl.
3. In another bowl beat eggs, and mix in water.
4. Toss the okra in the egg mix.
5. Strain okra then add to flour mixture and toss to coat.
6. Cook at 320 degrees for 10 minutes.

Nutritional Info: Calories: 198, Sodium: 1004 mg, Dietary Fiber: 6.2 g, Total Fat: 1.5 g, Total Carbs: 38.2 g, Protein: 8.2 g.

Fried Brussels Sprouts

Servings: 4 | Prep Time: 5 Minutes | Cook Time: 10 Minutes

This simple recipe may literally change your life. Not many people enjoy the taste of Brussels sprouts, even though they are incredible good for you. This recipe turns soggy old sprouts into crisp leaves with a lightly seasoned taste.

Ingredients:

1 pound brussels sprouts, stems removed and cut in half

4 tablespoons flour

Salt and pepper to taste

Instructions:

1. Cut the Brussels sprouts in half.
2. Pour flour into a bowl and mix in salt and pepper to taste.
3. Toss sprouts in flour and put into basket.
4. Air-fry at 320 degrees for 10 minutes tossing regularly.

Nutritional Info: Calories: 77, Sodium: 29 mg, Dietary Fiber: 4.5 g, Total Fat: 0.5 g, Total Carbs: 16.3 g, Protein: 4.7 g.

Crispy Cauliflower

Servings: 4 | Prep Time: 5 Minutes | Cook Time: 10 Minutes

This crispy cauliflower recipe offers the best of both worlds with a nice crisp outside and a soft, creamy inside. It has a nice mild flavor making it a family favorite and a perfect side to pair with many recipes.

Ingredients:

3-4 cups cauliflower florets

1 cup coconut cream

1/2 cup panko crumbs

1/2 cup polenta

1 teaspoon ground turmeric

1 teaspoon ground cumin

1/2 teaspoon salt

1/4 teaspoon chili powder

Instructions:

1. Place coconut cream in a bowl.

2. In a second bowl, combine panko, polenta, turmeric, cumin, salt, and chili powder.

3. Dip the cauliflower in the coconut cream, and roll in the panko mixture until coated evenly.

4. Cook at 320 degrees in your Philips air fryer for 10 minutes, shaking often.

Nutritional Info: Calories: 284, Sodium: 423 mg, Dietary Fiber: 4.6 g, Total Fat: 15.5 g, Total Carbs: 33 g, Protein: 6.3 g.

Fried Bread

Servings: 2 | Prep Time: 35 Minutes | Cook Time 20 Minutes

Fried bread is great for a snack or side, but traditional fried bread comes with a hefty side of guilt. This recipe forgoes any oil and leaves you with a crispy, flaky bread without all of the grease.

Ingredients:

1 cup all-purpose flour

1 teaspoon baking powder

1/8 teaspoon salt

1/3 cup hot water

Instructions:

1. In a medium mixing bowl mix together flour, salt, and baking powder.

2. Stir in hot water, cover with a towel, and let sit for 30 minutes.

3. Divide the dough and roll it into 6 inch circles.

4. Cook using Philips at 320 degrees for 20 minutes.

Nutritional Info: Calories: 230, Sodium: 152 mg, Dietary Fiber: 1.8 g, Total Fat: 0.6 g, Total Carbs: 48.9 g, Protein: 6.5 g.

Nut Butter Crusted Parsnip Fries

Servings: 2 | Prep Time: 10 Minutes | Cook Time: 30 Minutes

These are a delicious and healthy alternative to traditional French fries. They have a nice crisp texture as well as a rich taste which make them a great side item or even a nice snack.

Ingredients:

3 medium parsnips, peeled and cut into thin fry-like strips

3 tablespoons nut butter

1 tablespoon extra-virgin olive oil

1/4 teaspoons sea salt, or to taste

Instructions:

1. Cut parsnips into fries.
2. Mix the rest of the ingredients in a bowl.
3. Toss the parsnips in the nut butter mix.
4. Air-fry using Philips at 400 degrees for 30 minutes, tossing regularly.

Nutritional Info: Calories: 251, Sodium: 351 mg, Dietary Fiber: 16.7 g, Total Fat: 19.3 g, Total Carbs: 16.7 g, Protein: 6.8 g.

8

Vegan / Vegetarian Recipes

Broccoli Fritters

Servings: 4 | Prep Time: 10 Minutes | Cook Time: 20 Minutes

This recipe does not go full vegan, but it is a nice vegetarian recipe which can be used on its own or to replace a meat patty. It offers a nice even flavor that is sure to please the pallet of even the pickiest eater at your dinner table.

Ingredients:

8 ounces steamed broccoli

1 large egg

1/2 cup all-purpose flour

1/3 cup finely grated parmesan cheese

1 small clove garlic

1/2 teaspoon sea salt, plus more to taste

A pinch of red pepper flakes or several grinds of black pepper

Instructions:

1. Beat the egg in a large mixing bowl.
2. Add flour, cheese, garlic, salt, and pepper; mix well.
3. Add the broccoli to the bowl and use a potato masher (a fork will work if you don't have one) to mash it into small pieces.
4. Mix everything together until the batter is even and pour even amounts into a muffin tin.
5. Bake in your Philips air fryer at 360 degrees for 20 minutes.

Nutritional Info: Calories: 581, Sodium: 1734 mg, Dietary Fiber: 1.9 g, Total Fat: 33.9 g, Total Carbs: 21.5 g, Protein: 53.4 g.

California Fried Walnuts

Servings: 16 | Prep Time: 10 Minutes | Cook Time: 5 Minutes

These walnuts are a masterpiece and could be categorized as a snack or desert. No matter how you look at them they are a healthy option that is sure to please almost anyone.

Ingredients:

6 cups water

4 cups walnut halves

1/2 cup sugar

1-1/4 teaspoon salt

Instructions:

1. Bring water to boil in a large sauce pan.

2. Add walnuts and boil for 1 minute

3. Drain and rinse the walnuts, then transfer to a bowl and toss in sugar.

4. Cook at 350 degrees for 5 minutes tossing halfway through.

5. Sprinkle with salt and serve.

Nutritional Info: Calories: 217, Sodium: 38 mg, Dietary Fiber: 2.1 g, Total Fat: 18.4 g, Total Carbs: 9.3 g, Protein: 7.5 g.

Crispy Buffalo Cauliflower

Servings: 5 | Prep Time: 10 Minutes | Cook Time: 15 Minutes

This recipe is so delicious and so comparable to traditional buffalo wings that it may even turn me into a vegan. It offers all of the taste and texture without any of the guilt which, in my humble opinion, makes it one of the best vegan recipes ever.

Ingredients:

- 1/2 cup cornstarch
- 1/2 cup all-purpose flour
- 1/2 teaspoon baking powder
- Sea salt
- 1/2 cup cold water
- 1/2 cup vodka
- 1 head cauliflower, cut into 1-inch florets
- 1/3 cup hot sauce
- 1 medium clove minced garlic
- 1 tablespoon olive oil

Instructions:

1. Combine flour, corn starch, 2 teaspoons salt, and baking soda into a bowl and mix until even.
2. Add water and vodka to the mix and stir until creating a batter.
3. Dip cauliflower florets into the batter and place in the basket.
4. Using your Philips, cook at 360 degrees for 15 minutes, shaking often.
5. While the florets cook, combine hot sauce, garlic, and olive oil.
6. Toss cauliflower in hot sauce mix and serve.

Nutritional Info: Calories: 186, Sodium: 612 mg, Dietary Fiber: 1.9 g, Total Fat: 3.0 g, Total Carbs: 24.7 g, Protein: 2.5 g.

Crispy Salt and Pepper Tofu

Servings: 4 | Prep Time: 35 Minutes | Cook Time: 18 Minutes

This recipe is so simple, yet it makes such a bland food stand out. The slight pop of flavor with the salt and peppercorn combined with a crispy outside is enough to turn even the most stalwart meat eater into a tofu lover.

Ingredients:

1 pack (1/2 pound) of firm tofu

1/4 cup corn flour

2 teaspoons black peppercorns

1 teaspoon rock salt

Instructions:

1. Start by draining the tofu as much as possible, up to half an hour if you have time. Simply open the package and leave it on a stack of paper towels.

2. Cut the tofu into 1 inch by 1 inch cubes.

3. Grind the salt and pepper with a pestle and mortar.

4. Pour corn flour and salt and pepper mix into a sealable bag and shake well.

5. Add tofu cubes to the bag and shake well to coat the tofu.

6. Cook at 360 degrees for 18 minutes, shaking regularly.

Nutritional Info: Calories: 69, Sodium: 248 mg, Dietary Fiber: 1.3 g, Total Fat: 2.7 g, Total Carbs: 7.3 g, Protein: 5.3 g.

Fried Artichokes

Servings: 8 | Prep Time: 15 Minutes | Cook Time: 10 Minutes

Artichokes have a unique taste which sets off many dishes. This particular recipe allows artichokes to take center stage and become the desirable dish they have always wanted to be.

Ingredients:

2 tablespoons fine sea salt

1 teaspoon ground black pepper

Juice and rind of 2 lemons

8 american globe artichokes

Instructions:

1. Fill a medium mixing bowl with water and add lemon juice and rinds and set aside.

2. Using a paring knife cut off as much of the hard outer shell that you can and trim the stem down to about 2 inches.

3. Immediate place the artichokes in the lemon water to prevent the artichokes from browning.

4. Dry artichokes with a paper towel and sprinkle with salt and pepper.

5. Cook in your Philips at 350 degrees for 10 minutes shaking often.

6. Remove artichokes from basket and place them on their heads.

7. Spoon out the choke and serve.

Nutritional Info: Calories: 81, Sodium: 1557 mg, Dietary Fiber: 9.2 g, Total Fat: 0.3 g, Total Carbs: 18.6 g, Protein: 5.5 g.

Fried Golden Fuyus

Servings: 4 | Prep Time: 10 Minutes | Cook Time: 10 Minutes

These are an awesome snack for any occasion and the fact that they are a vegan option makes them even better. They are relatively quick and easy to make which is important for busy families.

Ingredients:

4 small ripe fuyu persimmons

1 1/2 cups organic panko bread crumbs

1/2 cup whole wheat flour

1/2 cup soy milk

2 tablespoons maple syrup

1 tablespoon cinnamon

1 teaspoon fresh citrus juice

Instructions:

1. Cut each end off of your fuyu, then slice them into 1/4 inch circles.

2. Combine soy milk and syrup in a shallow dish, mix well.

3. Put your panko crumbs on a flat plate.

4. Mix together your flour and cinnamon in another shallow bowl.

5. Dip each circle in the milk bowl, then flour, then milk again, then press each side into panko crumbs.

6. Cook at 360 degrees for 10 minutes, flipping half way through. Squeeze citrus juice over the fruyus and serve.

Nutritional Info: Calories: 69, Sodium: 248 mg, Dietary Fiber: 1.3 g, Total Fat: 2.7 g, Total Carbs: 7.3 g, Protein: 5.3 g.

Fried Plantains

Servings: 3 | Prep Time: 1 Hour 5 Minutes | Cook Time: 10 Minutes

This recipe proves that there are times when you are allowed to have your cake and eat it too. This recipe is relatively healthy, but your taste buds would never that.

Ingredients:

2 ripe plantains

1 cup panko bread crumbs

1/2 cup orange juice

Instructions:

1. Peel plantains and cut them into 1/4-inch-thick circles.
2. Pour orange juice into a bowl and soak plantain slices in the orange juice for at least an hour in the fridge.
3. Toss slices in panko until covered evenly and place in basket.
4. Cook at 320 degrees for 10 minutes, tossing a few times.

Nutritional Info: Calories: 306, Sodium: 269 mg, Dietary Fiber: 4.4 g, Total Fat: 2.4 g, Total Carbs: 68.3 g, Protein: 6.6 g.

Gobi

Servings: 4 | Prep Time: 1 Hour 15 Minutes | Cook Time: 15 Minutes

Gobi takes a lot of preparation, but the end results are worth it. The best part is that this vegan recipe has more flavor to it than most meat dishes could dream of.

Ingredients:

Main ingredient:

3 cups small to medium cauliflower florets	enough hot water for covering florets

Red paste:

4 dry red chilies soaked in hot water	1 1/2 teaspoons roughly chopped ginger
1 1/2 teaspoons chopped garlic	1 to 2 tablespoons water for grinding to paste

Batter:

6 tablespoons besan	1/2 teaspoon garam masala powder
4 tablespoons rice flour	
2 tablespoons corn starch	1/2 teaspoon coriander powder/dhania powder
1/4 teaspoon turmeric powder/haldi	1/2 teaspoon lemon juice
1/2 teaspoon red chili powder/lal mirch powder	1/3 cup water
	Salt to taste

Tempering:

2 teaspoons olive oil

1/2 teaspoon mustard seeds

1 small onion or 1/4 cup chopped onion or spring onion whites

3 to 4 garlics or 1 teaspoon finely chopped garlic

1/2-inch ginger or 1 teaspoon finely chopped ginger

3 to 4 green chilies, slit

2 to 3 dry red chilies

5 to 6 curry leaves/kadi patta

1 tablespoon chopped coriander leaves/dhania patta

Instructions:

1. Chop cauliflower into small pieces, rinse, and place into a bowl.
2. Cover the cauliflower in hot water and let stand for 20 minutes.
3. Place 4 red chilies in a small bowl and cover in hot water for 15 minutes.
4. In a pestle or grinder, combine 1 1/2 teaspoons chopped garlic, 1 1/2 teaspoons chopped ginger, and the soaked chilies.
5. Add 2 tablespoons of water and grind into a paste.
6. Drain the cauliflower and return to bowl.
7. Mix paste and cauliflower together.
8. Add besan, rice flour, and cornstarch to the mix and stir well.
9. Next, pour in turmeric, red chili powder, garam masala powder, and coriander powder into the mix and combine.
10. Finally, mix in lemon juice, salt, and 1/3 cup water.
11. Allow the mixture to marinate for 30 minutes.
12. Place a small spoonful of the mixture in the basket and repeat until the basket has an even layer with small gaps between each spoonful.

13. Cook in your Philips at 320 degrees for 10 minutes, flipping the scoops halfway through.

14. While the mixture is marinating place 2 teaspoons of oil in a skillet and cook mustard seeds and remaining chilies together.

15. Mix in onion, garlic, ginger and curry leaves.

16. Add your fried cauliflower into the pan and turn off the heat.

17. Mix in coriander leaves and serve.

Nutritional Info: Calories: 158, Sodium: 72 mg, Dietary Fiber: 4.8 g, Total Fat: 3.6 g, Total Carbs: 27.9 g, Protein: 5.1 g.

Parsnip Fries

Servings: 4 | Prep Time: 10 Minutes | Cook Time: 15 Minutes

To be honest your kids will probably not even know that these aren't potato fries, but if they do catch on force them to try one. Pretty soon your kids will be begging to eat their vegetables and you will be more than happy to oblige.

Ingredients:

2 large or 4 medium parsnips

1 tablespoon avocado oil

Sea salt

Freshly ground pepper

Instructions:

1. Peel parsnips and cut them into 1/2-inch-wide fries.
2. Toss parsnips in avocado oil, salt, and pepper.
3. Cook at 400 degrees for 15 minutes, shake well.

Nutritional Info: Calories: 30, Sodium: 42 mg, Dietary Fiber: 1.8 g, Total Fat: 0.5 g, Total Carbs: 6.2 g, Protein: 0.4 g.

Potato and Pea Patties

Servings: 4 | Prep Time: 1 Hour 15 Minutes | Cook Time: 15 Minutes

These patties are the perfect replacement for a recipe which calls for chicken patties. They have roughly the same texture and a bold taste which will compliment anything else served with the patties. f

Ingredients:

- 3/4 pounds sweet potatoes, preferably light-fleshed, baked and cooled
- 1/2 pound red boiling potatoes, scrubbed and quartered
- 1/2 cup finely chopped fresh cilantro leaves
- 2 tablespoons grape seed oil
- 1/2 teaspoon red pepper flakes
- 1 tablespoon coriander seeds
- 2 teaspoons cumin seeds
- 1/4 teaspoon cayenne pepper
- 2 teaspoons fresh lemon juice
- 1 cup frozen peas, thawed
- 1 cup panko or chickpea flour

Instructions:

1. Peel sweet potatoes and place in a large bowl.

2. Quarter and boil red potatoes until soft, then combine with sweet potatoes.

3. Mash the potatoes together, then stir in the cilantro.

4. Heat 2 tablespoons of oil in a medium skillet and mix in red pepper flakes, coriander, and cumin; heating for until cumin is browned.

5. Stir in cayenne pepper, then pour in potato mixture.

6. Stir in peas and cook until peas and potatoes are warm.

7. Pour mixture back into bowl and mix in lemon juice, set aside to cool.

8. Scoop 1/3 of the potato mixture into your hands, roll it into a ball, and repeat.

9. Roll each ball in your choice of panko or flour, then flatten into a patty, and place on a place.

10. Refrigerate for at least an hour.

11. When ready, cook in your Philips air fryer at 400 degrees for 15 minutes flipping half way through.

Nutritional Info: Calories: 836, Sodium: 28 mg, Dietary Fiber: 15.6 g, Total Fat: 59.7 g, Total Carbs: 68.8 g, Protein: 14.1 g.

Pumpkin and Chickpea Fritters

Servings: 4 | Prep Time: 10 Minutes | Cook Time: 20 Minutes

These vegetable fritters are awesome because they are 100% vegan and are a great option to replace normal meat patties. These fritters offer a nice combination of sweet and tangy which makes for a happy palate.

Ingredients:

1 can chickpeas, drained

1/2 cup organic canned pumpkin puree

1/4 cup hemp seeds

1 teaspoon garlic granules

2 teaspoons apple cider vinegar

A few dashes of pepper, cayenne and salt to taste

Instructions:

1. Combine the chickpeas and pumpkin in a large bowl and smash together.

2. Mix in the salt, pepper, garlic, and cayenne.

3. Mix in vinegar and hemp seeds.

4. Roll the mix into balls, then flatten and place in the basket.

5. Bake in your Philips at 360 degrees for 20 minutes.

Nutritional Info: Calories: 280, Sodium: 53 mg, Dietary Fiber: 10.7 g, Total Fat: 10.7 g, Total Carbs: 42.7 g, Protein: 14.8 g.

Rosemary Sweet Potato Fries

Servings: 2 | Prep Time: 1 hour 10 Minutes | Cook Time: 20 Minutes

Sweet potatoes and fresh rosemary are a match made in heaven and a perfect vegan side item. This recipe is bursting with flavor, and though the prep time is long, it is a straight forward recipe that is easy to perfect.

Ingredients:

2 medium sweet potatoes

1-2 tablespoons coconut oil

1 tablespoon fresh rosemary

Sea salt & pepper

Instructions:

1. Cut sweet potatoes into fries.
2. Soak the fries in a bowl of water for an hour.
3. Remove fries and pat dry with paper towels.
4. Put the fries in a dry bowl and add coconut oil, rosemary, salt, and pepper, and toss.
5. Cook at 400 degrees for 20 minutes, shaking often.

Nutritional Info: Calories: 197, Sodium: 478 mg, Dietary Fiber: 4.3 g, Total Fat: 10.6 g, Total Carbs: 24.7 g, Protein: 2.6 g.

Tofu Tater Tots

Servings: 6 | Prep Time: 40 Minutes | Cook Time: 18 Minutes

Who would have ever thought that tofu could actually make a recipe better? These tofu tater tots are like a meal rolled together, but could also be a perfect side item or appetizer.

Ingredients:

Tofu Tots:

1 pack (275g) firm tofu	3 tablespoons flour
1 1/4 pounds peeled all-purpose potatoes	1 teaspoon salt
	black pepper

Crumb Coat:

1 cup flour	1-2 cups panko crumbs
1 cup soy milk	

Instructions:

1. Start by draining the tofu as much as possible, up to half an hour if you have time. Simply open the package and leave it on a stack of paper towels.

2. Grate the tofu into a large mixing bowl.

3. Grate the potatoes into another bowl, then squeeze handfuls over the sink to reduce liquid. Place each handful into the tofu bowl.

4. Add flour, salt, and pepper into the bowl and mix all of the ingredients with your hands to really press them together.

5. Roll small portions of the mixture into tater tot shapes and place them on a baking sheet.

6. Place flour, soy milk, and panko in 3 separate bowls.

7. Roll each tot in flour, dip in soy milk, and roll in panko before placing them in the basket to cook.

8. Cook at 360 degrees for 18 minutes, shaking regularly.

Nutritional Info: Calories: 209, Sodium: 420 mg, Dietary Fiber: 3.6 g, Total Fat: 3.0 g, Total Carbs: 37.1 g, Protein: 9.2 g.

Vegan Egg Nog French Toast

Servings: 5 | Prep Time: 5 Minutes | Cook Time: 10 Minutes |

If you want to prove that veganism isn't all that bad, use this recipe. This recipe is obviously meant for breakfast, but it could also double as a sweet treat with or without syrup.

Ingredients:

10 slices bread, I used day old sourdough bread (5 large slices, halved)

1 1/4 cups vegan eggnog

2 tablespoons espresso

1/4 teaspoon nutmeg

1/4 teaspoon cinnamon

1/4 teaspoon orange zest

1/2 banana

2 teaspoons ground flax seeds

1/8 teaspoon vanilla extract

Instructions:

1. Place all ingredients except for bread in a blender and blend for 2 minutes.

2. Pour the mixture into a shallow bowl.

3. Add bread and soak for minute so the bread absorbs the mixture.

4. Cook in your Philips at 360 degrees for 10 minutes, flipping half way.

Nutritional Info: Calories: 150, Sodium: 158 mg, Dietary Fiber: 1.1 g, Total Fat: 5.7 g, Total Carbs: 20.9 g, Protein: 4.1 g.

Vegan Lemon Cupcakes

Servings: 12 | Prep Time: 15 Minutes | Cook Time: 20 Minutes

When you are vegan even enjoying a decent desert can be a pain because there is butter in everything. This recipe fixes that issue with vegan butter and delivers a delectable treat that people won't believe is vegan.

Ingredients:

- 3 tablespoons ground flaxseed meal + 1/4 cup water
- 1 1/2 cups whole wheat pastry flour, sifted
- 1 teaspoon baking powder
- 1/4 teaspoon salt
- 4 lemons, zested
- 1/2 cup Earth Balance Vegan Buttery Sticks, at room temperature

- 1 cup organic sugar
- 1 teaspoon vanilla extract
- 2-3 drops lemon essential oil 1 teaspoon lemon extract (optional)
- 1/2 cup unsweetened almond milk
- 1/4 cup freshly squeezed lemon juice

Frosting:

- 3/4 cups Earth Balance Vegan Buttery Sticks, at room temperature
- 1 teaspoon vanilla extract
- 1-2 tablespoons fresh lemon juice

- 3 - 3 1/2 cups powdered sugar (homemade sugar-free variety or regular)

Instructions:

1. Mix together flax meal and water and set aside to let gel.

2. In a separate bowl mix together flour, salt, and baking powder.

3. Zest lemon and set it aside.

4. Place buttery spread and sugar into a mixing bowl and beat until creamy.

5. Mix in the flax mixture until it is even mixed, then add lemon oil, lemon zest, and vanilla extract until mixed evenly with all of the other ingredients.

6. Pour half of your flour mix into the bowl and mix slowly.

7. Mix in milk and lemon juice, then add the rest of the flour mix and continue to mix for 2 minutes.

8. Fill cupcake liners with mixture and place them in a baking sheet.

9. Bake in your Philips for 20 minutes at 350 degrees.

10. While your cupcakes bake mix together the frosting.

11. Beat the butter until smooth and slowly add in powdered sugar until creamy.

12. Mix in the lemon juice and vanilla extract; refrigerate until ready to top cupcakes.

Nutritional Info: Calories: 132, Sodium: 60 mg, Dietary Fiber: 2.1 g, Total Fat: 1.0 g, Total Carbs: 28.7 g, Protein: 1.9 g.

Zucchini Patties

Servings: 4 | Prep Time: 10 Minutes | Cook Time: 15 Minutes |

This vegetarian option is not only for the vegetarian in the family. It is full of flavor, easy to make, and offers a nice alternative to the regular weekly fair.

Ingredients:

2 cups grated zucchini (one medium sized zucchini)

1/2 small onion

1 large egg

1/4 cup grated parmesan cheese

1/2 cup all-purpose flour

Salt and pepper

Instructions:

1. Grate zucchini onto a plate lined with paper towels in order to drain.
2. Transfer zucchini into a bowl and dice onion into a bowl.
3. Add parmesan, egg, and flour and mix well.
4. Add salt and pepper to taste.
5. Form the batter into balls, then press them into patties and place in basket.
6. Cook in your Philips at 400 degrees for 15 minutes, flipping halfway through.

Nutritional Info: Calories: 452, Sodium: 1075 mg, Dietary Fiber: 1.3 g, Total Fat: 25.6 g, Total Carbs: 19.2 g, Protein: 40.3 g.

9

Main Dish Recipes

Adobo Crusted Lamb Loin Chops

Servings: 4 | Prep Time: 1 Hour 10 Minutes | Cook Time: 15 Minutes

Lamb does not get the respect it deserves in the average kitchen. Lamb is a rich meat with its own distinct flavor and recipes like this one really help to bring that flavor out. If your family doesn't know that they are eating lamb, they will probably be head over heels about this dish.

Ingredients:

1 tablespoon fennel seed

1 tablespoon cumin seed

2 teaspoons coriander seed

2 teaspoons cracked pepper

1 1/2 teaspoons salt

2 teaspoons minced garlic cloves

2 teaspoons fresh oregano leaves

2 teaspoons lime zest

1/2 teaspoon fresh thyme

1/2 teaspoon fresh rosemary leaves

8 lamb loin chops, 1-inch thick

Instructions:

1. Throw fennel, cumin, coriander, and pepper in a dry skillet and cook on medium heat until aromatic.

2. Let cool then grind in a spice grinder or mortar.

3. Put ground mix into a bowl and mix in salt, lime zest, oregano, and garlic.

4. Next, mix in rosemary and thyme.

5. Rub each side of the lamb chop with the spice mix then cover and set in the fridge for one hour.

6. Cook at 360 degrees for 15 minutes, flipping half way through.

Nutritional Info: Calories: 751, Sodium: 1161 mg, Dietary Fiber: 1.6 g, Total Fat: 32.7 g, Total Carbs: 3.5 g, Protein: 100.8 g.

Almond Crusted Chicken Fingers

Servings: 4 | Prep Time: 10 Minutes | Cook Time: 15 Minutes

This recipe is low in fat and high in flavor. The almonds really set off the crunchiness and will make you completely forget about that old oil fried chicken.

Ingredients:

Canola oil cooking spray

1/2 cup sliced almonds

1/4 cup whole-wheat flour

1 1/2 teaspoons paprika

1/2 teaspoon garlic powder

1/2 teaspoon dry mustard

1/4 teaspoon salt

1/8 teaspoon freshly ground pepper

1 1/2 teaspoons extra-virgin olive oil

4 large egg whites

1 pound chicken tenders

Instructions:

1. Combine flour, almonds, paprika, dry mustard, garlic powder, salt, and pepper into a food processor and process until the almonds are fine and the paprika is evenly mixed.

2. Drizzle oil into the flour mixture and process for another minute.

3. Beat egg whites in a shallow bowl.

4. Coat chicken tenders in egg, then coat evenly in flour mixture.

5. Cook in your Philips air fryer at 360 degrees for 15 minutes, flipping the chicken halfway through.

Nutritional Info: Calories: 352, Sodium: 279 mg, Dietary Fiber: 2.1 g, Total Fat: 16.5 g, Total Carbs: 9.6 g, Protein: 40 g.

Asian Pork Chops

Servings: 4 | Prep Time: 2 Hours 10 Minutes | Cook Time: 15 Minutes

These sweet pork chops are an excellent meal for midweek or Friday night. They are sure to be a family favorite and would definitely pair well with a nice wine.

Ingredients:

1/2 cup hoisin sauce

3 tablespoons cider vinegar

1 tablespoon Asian sweet chili sauce

1/4 teaspoon garlic powder

4 (1/2-inch-thick) boneless pork chops

1 teaspoon salt

1/2 teaspoon pepper

Instructions:

1. Stir together hoisin, chili sauce, garlic powder, and vinegar in a large mixing bowl.

2. Separate 1/4 cup of this mixture, then add pork chops to the bowl and marinate in the fridge for 2 hours.

3. Remove the pork chops and place them on a plate.

4. Sprinkle each side of the pork chop evenly with salt and pepper.

5. Cook at 360 degrees for 14 minutes, flipping half way through.

6. Brush with reserved marinade and serve.

Nutritional Info: Calories: 338, Sodium: 1185 mg, Dietary Fiber: 1.0 g, Total Fat: 21 g, Total Carbs: 16 g, Protein: 19.1 g.

Brown Sugar Brined Turkey

Servings: 6 | Prep Time: 12 Hours, 10 Minutes | Cook Time: 20 Minutes

This recipe may take a little planning, but the results are definitely worth it. You will be hard pressed to find a turkey recipe that is a bigger crowd pleaser than this one.

Ingredients:

3 cups packed light brown sugar

1 1/2 cups Dijon mustard

1/2 cup table salt

2 tablespoons cayenne pepper

2 gallons icy cold water

1 bunch fresh thyme

1 head fresh garlic, separated into cloves and crushed

1 (10-12 pounds) whole turkey, thawed

Instructions:

1. In a large cooking pot, mix together brown sugar, mustard, salt, and pepper.

2. Slowly mix in the water, thyme, and garlic.

3. Prep your turkey by removing anything you need including giblets and timer.

4. Place the turkey to the pot, cover, and refrigerate overnight.

5. When ready to cook, remove turkey from pot, drain, and rinse.

6. Cut turkey into pieces small enough to fit in the basket.

7. With your Philips air fryer, cook the turkey at 375 degrees for 20 minutes, turning half way through.

8. Given the size this will probably take several batches.

Nutritional Info: Calories: 1754, Sodium: 590 mg, Dietary Fiber: 6.5 g, Total Fat: 49.5 g, Total Carbs: 86.5 g, Protein: 231.7 g.

Country Fried Steak and Mushroom Gravy

Servings: 4 | Prep Time: 15 Minutes | Cook Time: 15 Minutes

There will never be a healthier and more flavorful way to cook a country fried steak than this. It is perfect to serve at any time of day and will definitely be a crowd pleaser.

Ingredients:

4 cubed steaks

2 large eggs

1/2 dozen mushrooms

4 tablespoons unsalted butter

4 tablespoons black pepper

2 tablespoons salt

1/2 teaspoon onion powder

1/2 teaspoon garlic powder

1/4 teaspoon cayenne powder

1 1/4 teaspoons paprika

1 1/2 cups whole milk

1/3 cup flour

2 tablespoons vegetable oil

Instructions:

1. Mix 1/2 flour and a pinch of black pepper in a shallow bowl or on a plate.

2. Beat 2 eggs in a bowl and mix in a pinch of salt and pepper.

3. In another shallow bowl mix together the other half of the flour with a pepper to taste, garlic powder, paprika, cayenne, and onion powder.

4. Chop mushrooms and set aside.

5. Press your steak into the first flour bowl, then dip in egg, then press the steak into the second flour bowl until covered completely.

6. Cook steak in your Philips at 360 degrees for 15 Minutes, flipping halfway through.

7. While the steak cooks, warm the butter over medium heat and add mushrooms to sauté.

8. Add 4 tablespoons of the flour and pepper mix to the pan and mix until there are no clumps of flour.

9. Mix in whole milk and simmer.

10. Serve over steak for breakfast, lunch, or dinner.

Nutritional Info: Calories: 442, Sodium: 477 mg, Dietary Fiber: 2.3 g, Total Fat: 27.5 g, Total Carbs: 17.4 g, Protein: 31.8 g.

Crispy Fried Pork Cutlets

Servings: 4 | Prep Time: 10 Minutes | Cook Time: 14 Minutes

This is an easy way to take an already tasty dish and make it even better. Crispy pork is not as common as it should be because the crispy outside really takes pork cutlets to the next level.

Ingredients:

1 1/2 cups panko bread crumbs

1/2 cup grated parmesan

Sea salt

11 (1/4-pound) pork tenderloin, sliced 3/4 inches thick, pounded 1/4 inch thick

2 eggs

Instructions:

1. Beat the eggs in a bowl and set aside.
2. In a separate bowl mix together panko, 1/2 teaspoon salt, and parmesan; once completely mixed pour on to a plate.
3. Dip the pork cutlets in egg, then press into panko mix on each side to coat evenly.
4. Cook at 360 degrees for 14 minutes, flipping halfway through.

Nutritional Info: Calories: 2,745, Sodium: 3160 mg, Dietary Fiber: 1.8 g, Total Fat: 97.7 g, Total Carbs: 37.4 g, Protein: 414.9 g.

Easy Fried Fish Filets

Servings: 4 | Prep Time: 5 Minutes | Cook Time: 15 Minutes

These fried fish filets are the perfect marriage of delicious, easy, and healthy. Their light texture and full flavor make them perfect to pair with many side dishes.

Ingredients:

1 pound fish fillets, such as haddock, tilapia, cod, etc.

1/2 cup flour

Salt and pepper to taste

1/4 teaspoon paprika

Instructions:

1. In a single bowl, combine flour, salt, pepper, and paprika.
2. Evenly coat each filet in the flour mix, then lay the filets in a single layer in the basket.
3. Cook in your Philips at 360 degrees for 15 minutes, flip the filets halfway through.

Nutritional Info: Calories: 120, Sodium: 89 mg, Dietary Fiber: 0 g, Total Fat: 1.0 g, Total Carbs: 0.1 g, Protein: 25.9 g.

Easy Indian Fish Fry

Servings: 3 | Prep Time: 25 Minutes | Cook Time: 15 Minutes

If you are a fan of Indian food, you will be a fan of this recipe. It has all of the flavor and spice that Indian food is known for and it relatively easy to prepare when it comes to this type of food. You also get the added benefit of Omega-3 rich fish for dinner.

Ingredients:

1 pound fish fillets

First Marinade:

1 tablespoon ginger garlic paste or coarsely crushed

Lemon juice as needed

Salt as needed

1/3 teaspoon turmeric

3/4 teaspoons garam masala

1/2 teaspoon coriander powder

1/2 teaspoon red chili powder

Second Marinade:

1 1/2 tablespoons rice flour

1 1/2 tablespoons besan / chickpea flour / gram flour

Salt as needed

1/4 teaspoon paprika

1/2 teaspoon saunf

1/2 teaspoon ajwain

1/4 teaspoon Kasuri methi or 1 sprig curry leaves chopped finely

Instructions:

1. Mix all the ingredients under the first marinade together.

2. Wash the fish filets and pat dry with a paper towel.

3. Place filets in marinade one and set aside for 15 minutes

4. While the filets marinate, combine ajwain and saunf together and grind into powder.

5. Mix the powder with the rest of the ingredients mentioned under the second marinade (flour mix).

6. Coat the fish evenly in the flour mix and set aside for 5 minutes to allow the flour mix to stick to the fish.

7. Cook in your Philips at 360 degrees for 15 minutes, flip the filets halfway through.

Nutritional Info: Calories: 227, Sodium: 124 mg, Dietary Fiber: 1.0 g, Total Fat: 4.5 g, Total Carbs: 8.8 g, Protein: 35.6 g.

Fried Chicken Livers

Servings: 4 | Prep Time: 5 Minutes | Cook Time: 10 Minutes

Most people shutter at the idea of liver but this recipe will have them changing their tune. This dish is super easy to make and about as delicious as they come.

Ingredients:

1 pound chicken livers

1 cup flour

1/2 cup cornmeal

2 teaspoons your favorite seasoning blend

3 eggs

2 tablespoons milk

Instructions:

1. Clean and rinse the livers, pat dry.
2. Beat eggs in a shallow bowl and mix in milk.
3. In another bowl combine flour, cornmeal, and seasoning, mixing until even.
4. Dip the livers in the egg mix, then toss them in the flour mix.
5. Air-fry at 375 degrees for 10 minutes using your Philips. Toss at least once halfway through.

Nutritional Info: Calories: 409, Sodium: 142 mg, Dietary Fiber: 2.0 g, Total Fat: 11.7 g, Total Carbs: 37.2 g, Protein: 36.6 g.

Fried Chicken Sandwich

Servings: 4 | Prep Time: 10 Minutes | Cook Time: 15 Minutes

There is a reason why almost every restaurant in the country has a fried chicken sandwich on their menu. Something about crispy chicken is just a universal draw. With this recipe, you get all of the taste with a fraction of the calories of those restaurant sandwiches.

Ingredients:

4 small skinless, boneless chicken thighs

3/4 cups low-fat buttermilk

2 teaspoons garlic powder

1/2 teaspoon salt

1/2 teaspoon pepper

1 cup all-purpose flour

4 potato rolls

Shredded romaine

Sliced tomatoes

Sliced pickles

Hot sauce

Instructions:

1. Place your chicken in a large bowl and mix in buttermilk, garlic powder, salt, and pepper.

2. Place the flour in a separate bowl.

3. Pull the chicken out of the buttermilk mix, letting excess drip off, cover in flour, dip in buttermilk mix, then cover in flour again.

4. Using your Philips air fryer, cook at 360 degrees for 15 minutes, flipping the chicken halfway through.

5. Serve on a potato roll with lettuce, tomatoes, pickles, and hot sauce.

Nutritional Info: Calories: 393, Sodium: 386 mg, Dietary Fiber: 4.8 g, Total Fat: 4.4 g, Total Carbs: 56.9 g, Protein: 30.8 g.

Fried Fish Tacos

Servings: 8 | Prep Time: 5 Minutes | Cook Time: 15 Minutes

Fish tacos are becoming increasingly popular for many reasons from street tacos to high class restaurants. Now you can make fish tacos at home that satisfy the palate of the kids and the sensibilities of mom and dad.

Ingredients:

2 pounds cod	*16 soft tortillas*
3 cups panko breadcrumbs	*1 (14 ounce) bag Coleslaw*
3 eggs	*2 avocados*
2 teaspoons cold water	*1 tomatoes*
Salt and pepper to taste	

Instructions:

1. Beat eggs, water, salt, and pepper together in a bowl.
2. Pour your bread crumbs into a separate bowl.
3. Cut fish into 8 pieces and season with salt and paper.
4. Dip fish in egg mixture, then roll in panko crumbs to coat evenly.
5. Place them on a pan lined with paper towels to allow the bread crumbs to soak into the fish.
6. Cook in your Philips at 360 degrees for 15 minutes, flipping halfway through.
7. Serve with tortillas, avocados, coleslaw, and tomatoes.

Nutritional Info: Calories: 586, Sodium: 567 mg, Dietary Fiber: 8.4 g, Total Fat: 21.5 g, Total Carbs: 62.0 g, Protein: 37.9 g.

Fried Haddock

Servings: 4 | Prep Time: 10 Minutes | Cook Time 15 Minutes

It is hard for most people to get their family to eat fish, but with delicious recipes like this one they will be begging for these fish filets. The fish comes out light and crispy instead of heavy and greasy which makes it just as healthy as it does delicious.

Ingredients:

3/4 cups milk

2 teaspoons salt

2 to 3 haddock fillets

3/4 cups plain, fine bread crumbs

1/4 cup grated parmesan cheese

1/4 teaspoon dried leaf thyme

Paprika

Parsley sprigs

Lemon wedges

Instructions:

1. Mix the milk and salt in a shallow bowl.

2. In another bowl mix together the bread crumbs, thyme, and parmesan.

3. Dip each Haddock filet in the milk mixture then toss it in the bread crumb mix until fully coated.

4. Cook in your Philips at 360 degrees for 15 minutes, flip the filets halfway through.

5. Sprinkle paprika over the filets while they cool and garnish with parsley and lemon.

Nutritional Info: Calories: 196, Sodium: 254 mg, Dietary Fiber: 1.2 g, Total Fat: 1.2 g, Total Carbs: 17.4 g, Protein: 23.1 g.

Fried Polenta and Mushroom Ragu

Servings: 6 | Prep Time: 3 Hours 5 Minutes | Cook Time: 10 Minutes

This is a great recipe to usher in the fall. It is a little labor intensive but the rich texture and flavor are worth the work and the wait.

Ingredients:

4 cups water

1 cup polenta

Sea salt

1/2 cup finely grated parmesan cheese

2 tablespoons olive oil

1 small yellow onion, diced

3 cloves garlic, minced

1 pound mixed wild mushrooms (shiitake, oyster, chanterelle, hen of the woods, etc.), cleaned and sliced

1 pound cremini mushrooms, cleaned and sliced

1 tablespoon minced fresh thyme

2 tablespoons of flour

1/2 cup dry white wine

1/4 cup heavy cream

1 teaspoon sugar

Squeeze of lemon juice to taste

1/2 cup chopped flat leaf parsley

Instructions:

1. Boil for cups up water and mix in polenta, reduce to medium heat and cook for 45 minutes stirring occasionally.

2. Stir in 1/4 teaspoon salt and parmesan; remove from heat.

3. Line a baking dish and pour in polenta mix, refrigerate for 2 hours.

4. While polenta cools, heat oil over medium heat and add mushroom and garlic to sauté.

5. Add in mushrooms and thyme and cook for about 5 minutes.

6. Stir in salt and cook for an additional 5 minutes.

7. Stir in flour and cook for another minute.

8. Stir in wine, cream, and sugar and simmer for about 10 minutes.

9. Add in a squeeze of lemon juice and parsley, then set aside and cover.

10. Slice your polenta into squares and place it in the Philips air fryer basket.

11. Cook at 360 degrees for 10 minutes, flipping halfway through.

12. Cover with mushroom ragu and serve.

Nutritional Info: Calories: 232, Sodium: 70 mg, Dietary Fiber: 2.6 g, Total Fat: 7.7 g, Total Carbs: 31.5 g, Protein: 7.7 g.

Fried Ravioli

Servings: 6 | Prep Time: 5 Minutes | Cook Time: 10 Minutes

One of the benefits of this recipe is that it can be served right away or frozen to be served at a later date. There is nothing out of this world about this recipe it is a great standby with a slight twist which makes it just that much better.

Ingredients:

1/2 cup unbleached all-purpose flour

2 eggs

1 cup panko breadcrumbs

1 cup dry breadcrumbs

48 fresh cheese raviolis

Salt

Instructions:

1. Place the flour in a shallow bowl and the panko in a separate shallow bowl.

2. Lightly beat the eggs in a third bowl.

3. Take your ravioli (we suggest store bought) and toss it in flour, dip it in egg, and press it in panko until fully coated.

4. Cook in your Philips at 360 degrees for 10 minutes.

Nutritional Info: Calories: 1104, Sodium: 1702 mg, Dietary Fiber: 1.9 g, Total Fat: 77.7 g, Total Carbs: 36.9 g, Protein: 63.5 g.

Fried Scallops

Servings: 12 | Prep Time: 5 Minutes | Cook Time: 10 Minutes

Scallops are not for everyone, but this recipe helps to make them more appealing. This recipe is super simple, super quick, and yields many servings making it a great option for party fair.

Ingredients:

1 cup white flour

1 cup fine corn meal

1 teaspoon baking powder

4 pounds scallops, under 10 to 12 to a pound, preferably dry

Instructions:

1. Combine flour, corn flour, and baking power in a medium bowl.

2. Pat scallops dry, then toss in flour mix.

3. Cook at 375 degrees for 10 minutes, shaking a few times.

Nutritional Info: Calories: 211, Sodium: 244 mg, Dietary Fiber: 1.3 g, Total Fat: 1.6 g, Total Carbs: 20.7 g, Protein: 27.5 g.

Fried Squid with Aioli

Servings: | Prep Time: 40 Minutes | Cook Time: 10 Minutes

Some people may shudder at the thought of eating squid, but they have never tried this recipe. It offers the flavor of squid that some people like, but not so overpowering that it turns you off from enjoying squid. Plus; how often do you have a chance to make your own aioli?

Ingredients

2/3 cups potato starch

1 1/4 teaspoons baking powder

1 3/4 cups arepa flour

1 large egg yolk

1 garlic clove, finely grated

1 teaspoon fresh lemon juice

1/2 cup grapeseed oil

1/4 cup olive oil

Sea salt

6 ounces cleaned squid, bodies and tentacles separated

4 scallions, white and pale-green parts only, sliced into 3-inch pieces

4 very thin lemon wheels

1/3 cup torn basil leaves

Instructions:

1. In a large bowl, mix the 3/4 cups arepa flour, baking powder, and potato starch together.

2. Mix 2 1/3 cups water into the arepa flour mix and allow it to sit for half an hour.

3. Place the remaining arepa flour in a separate shallow bowl.

4. While the arepa flour mix is hydrating mix the egg yolk, lemon juice, and garlic in a separate bowl.

5. Continue to stir the egg yolk mix while slowly pouring in the grapeseed and olive oils. Keep stirring until the sauce thickens – this is your aioli.

6. Season the aioli with salt and add a teaspoon of water to make it ready to serve.

7. Cut your squid into triangular chunks that are about 1 1/2 inches wide at the bottom.

8. Rinse the chunks and pat them down with a dry paper towel.

9. Coat the squid, lemon slices, and scallions in the plain arepa flour and then in the arepa flour batter mix.

10. Cook them in batches in your Philips air fryer at 360 degrees for about 10 minutes, tossing half way through.

11. Top with basil and serve with your home made aioli sauce.

Nutritional Info: Calories: 945, Sodium: 33 mg, Dietary Fiber: 3.9 g, Total Fat: 42.7 g, Total Carbs: 121.3 g, Protein: 18.2 g.

Fried Stuffed Oysters on the Half Shell with Crawfish Stuffing

Servings: 8 | Prep Time: 15 Minutes | Cook Time: 10 Minutes

If you are into oysters, you are going to love this recipe. It is definitely an acquired taste, but for seafood junkies this recipe is a dream come true.

Ingredients:

Crawfish Stuffing:

4 ounces olive oil

1 1/2 cups onion, finely chopped

1 1/2 cups bell pepper, finely chopped

2 tablespoons fresh garlic, minced

1 pound crawfish tails, chopped

1 teaspoon blackened seasoning

1/2 teaspoon Cajun seasoning

2 ounces garlic sauce

1/4 cup fresh parsley, finely chopped

1/4 cup green onions, minced

1 1/2 cups plain breadcrumbs

Oysters:

24 oysters on the half shell

2 cups all-purpose flour

2 cups buttermilk

2 ounces Cajun seasoning

1 package fried fish mix

111

Instructions:

1. Place butter in skillet, then add onions, bell pepper, and garlic and sauté.

2. Add crawfish tails and cook for 3 minutes.

3. Mix in blackened and Cajun spices.

4. Remove the mix from heat and stir in garlic sauce.

5. Stir in parsley, onion, and bread crumbs until crumbs begin to moisten.

6. Wash and shuck oysters, leaving them on the half shell.

7. Stuff each oyster with the crawfish mix.

8. Place flour and fried fish mix in 2 separate bowls.

9. In a 3rd bowl mix together buttermilk and Cajun seasoning.

10. Press oysters in flour, dip in buttermilk, then press in fish mix to coat.

11. Cook at 360 degrees for 10 minutes in your Philips.

Nutritional Info: Calories: 405.4 g, Sodium: 463.9 mg, Dietary Fiber: 2.8 g, Total Fat: 16 g, Total Carbs: 46 g, Protein: 19 g.

Fried Tortellini

Servings: 3 | Prep Time: 10 Minutes | Cook Time: 10 Minutes

This recipe takes and already delicious food and brings it to another level. You get all of the cheesy goodness that you expect from tortellini along with a new experience of a crispy and flavorful outer shell.

Ingredients:

1 cup all-purpose flour

4 eggs

1 cup Italian style bread crumbs

3/4 cups parmesan cheese

3 tablespoons all-purpose seasoning

1 tablespoon dried parsley

3 tablespoons granulated garlic

2 teaspoons salt

1 teaspoon pepper

1 -20 ounces packet fresh herb chicken tortellini

Instructions:

1. Place your flour into a shallow dish.
2. Beat eggs into a separate shallow dish.
3. Put seasoning, salt, pepper, parsley, garlic, cheese, and breadcrumbs into a large freezer bag.
4. Roll tortellini in flour, dip in egg, and place into seasoning bag.
5. Zip freezer bag and toss until tortellini is completely coated.
6. Cook at 360 degrees for 10 minutes, shaking often.

Nutritional Info: Calories: 1388, Sodium: 3420 mg, Dietary Fiber: 2.4 g, Total Fat: 79 g, Total Carbs: 58.3 g, Protein: 122.2 g.

Indian Fish Fingers

Servings: 4 | Prep Time: 35 Minutes | Cook Time: 15 Minutes

These work just as well as a main course as they do as a snack. They offer just enough spice and the perfect mixture of soft and crispy that will make you crave fish.

Ingredients:

1/2 pound fish fillet

1 tablespoon finely chopped fresh mint leaves or any fresh herbs

1/3 cup bread crumbs

1 teaspoon ginger garlic paste or ginger and garlic powders

1 hot green chili finely chopped

1/2 teaspoon paprika

Generous pinch of black pepper

Salt to taste

3/4 tablespoons lemon juice

3/4 teaspoons garam masala powder

1/3 teaspoon rosemary

1 egg

Instructions:

1. Start by removing any skin on the fish, washing, and patting dry.
2. Cut the fish into fingers.
3. In a medium bowl mix together all ingredients except for fish, mint, and bread crumbs.
4. Bury the fingers in the mixture and refrigerate for 30 minutes.
5. Remove from the bowl from the fridge and mix in mint leaves.
6. In a separate bowl beat the egg, pour bread crumbs into a third bowl.
7. Dip the fingers in the egg bowl then toss them in the bread crumbs bowl.

8. Cook at 360 degrees for 15 minutes, toss the fingers halfway through.

Nutritional Info: Calories: 187, Sodium: 439 mg, Dietary Fiber: 1.0 g, Total Fat: 8.6 g, Total Carbs: 16.8 g, Protein: 11.0 g.

Japanese Style Fried Shrimp

Servings: 4 | Prep Time: 10 minutes | Cook Time: 10 minutes

These fried shrimp are different enough to be in their own category, but not so different that they will scare away the picky eater. Unlike other fried shrimp, which is pretty much just shrimp and batter, these combine a host of flavor to satisfy the palate. Fast prep and cook times make this recipe perfect for a weeknight family meal.

Ingredients:

1 pound medium shrimp, peeled (tails left on) and deveined

1/2 teaspoon salt

1/2 teaspoon ground black pepper

1/2 teaspoon garlic powder

1 cup all-purpose flour

1 teaspoon paprika

2 eggs

1 cup panko crumbs

Instructions:

1. Place your shrimp in a bowl and sprinkle it with the salt, pepper, and garlic powder.

2. In another bowl mix together the flour and the paprika.

3. Beat the eggs into another separate bowl and put the panko crumbs in their own bowl.

4. Dip each shrimp into the flour, then the egg mix, and roll in the panko crumbs until completely covered.

5. Cook at 375 degrees in your Philips for 10 minutes, shaking a few times.

Nutritional Info: Calories: 363, Sodium: 777 mg, Dietary Fiber: 2.4 g, Total Fat: 5.4 g, Total Carbs: 44.2 g, Protein: 34.1 g.

Old Bay Crab Cakes

Servings: 4 | Prep Time: 10 Minutes | Cook Time: 20 Minutes

Who doesn't love crab cakes? They can be used as an appetizer or a main course and they are bursting with that unmistakable crabby flavor. Try these out as crab burgers for something a little different.

Ingredients:

2 slices dried bread, crusts removed

Small amount of milk

1 tablespoon mayonnaise

1 tablespoon Worcestershire sauce

1 tablespoon baking powder

1 tablespoon parsley flakes

1 teaspoon Old Bay® Seasoning

1/4 teaspoon salt

1 egg

1 pound lump crabmeat

Instructions:

1. Crush your bread over a large bowl until it is broken down into small pieces.
2. Add milk and stir until bread crumbs are moistened.
3. Mix in mayo and Worcestershire sauce.
4. Add remaining ingredients and mix well.
5. Shape into 4 patties.
6. Cook at 360 degrees for 20 minutes, flip half way through.

Nutritional Info: Calories: 165, Sodium: 581 mg, Dietary Fiber: 0 g, Total Fat: 4.5 g, Total Carbs: 5.8 g, Protein: 24.7 g.

Oyster Sandwiches

Servings: 6 | Prep Time: 15 Minutes | Cook Time: 20 Minutes

Oyster sandwiches may not sound very appealing to some, but their taste buds will beg to differ. Not only is this recipe delicious, but it is fairly healthy too, which is a win-win. These sandwiches may not be every week thing, but they are definitely a nice treat.

Ingredients:

Spicy rémoulade sauce:

1 1/2 cups mayonnaise

1/4 cup whole-grain mustard

1 garlic clove, minced

1 tablespoon pickle juice

1 tablespoon drained capers

1 teaspoon horseradish

1/4 teaspoon cayenne pepper

1/4 teaspoon hot paprika

1/2 teaspoon hot sauce

Oysters:

1 cup buttermilk

Sea salt and freshly ground black pepper

48 oysters, shucked and drained

1 cup all-purpose flour

1/2 cup cornmeal

1/2 cup plain bread crumbs

2 tablespoons Old Bay Seasoning

6 brioches or potato hot dog rolls

Instructions:

1. Combine the mayo, hot sauce, mustard, garlic, pickle juice, capers, paprika, cayenne pepper, and horseradish; mix well.

2. Refrigerate until ready to serve.

3. Mix together the buttermilk, salt, and pepper.

4. Add oysters and let stand.

5. In another bowl, mix together flour, cornstarch, old bay spice, and bread crumbs.

6. Take the oysters out of the buttermilk mix and toss in the flour mix.

7. Using your Philips, cook at 360 degrees for 20 minutes, flipping half way through.

8. Serve inside of bun and topped with sauce.

Nutritional Info: Calories: 615, Sodium: 861.6 mg, Dietary Fiber: 3.8 g, Total Fat: 26.8 g, Total Carbs: 75.2 g, Protein: 18.3 g.

Potato Crusted Salmon

Servings: 4 | Prep Time: 10 Minutes | Cook Time: 15 Minutes

Salmon has a rather unique flavor that is not for everyone, but this recipe makes salmon a preferred dish. The crispy potato flakes compliment the taste of salmon with overpowering it completely.

Ingredients:

1 pound salmon, swordfish or arctic char fillets, 3/4 inch thick

1 egg white

2 tablespoons water

1/3 cup dry instant mashed potatoes

2 teaspoons cornstarch

1 teaspoon paprika

1 teaspoon lemon pepper seasoning

Instructions:

1. Remove and skin from the fish and cut it into 4 serving pieces.

2. Mix together the egg white and water.

3. Mix together all of the dry ingredients.

4. Dip the filets into the egg white mixture then press into the potato mix to coat evenly.

5. In your Philips, cook at 360 degrees for 15 minutes, flip the filets halfway through.

Nutritional Info: Calories: 176, Sodium: 63 mg, Dietary Fiber: 0.6 g, Total Fat: 7.1 g, Total Carbs: 5.2 g, Protein: 23.4 g.

Prawn and Mango Spring Rolls

Servings: 4 | Prep Time: 10 Minutes | Cook Time: 10 Minutes

These bad boys basically dance all over your taste buds from the tip of the tongue to the back of the throat. There is a little bit of work that goes into these, but they are still fairly simple to create and cook.

Ingredients:

6 large egg roll wrappers

1 large egg

12 large prawns

12 (3" long) peeled slices of fresh mango

24 to 36 small sprigs cilantro

Instructions:

1. Beat the egg in a bowl.

2. Cut each egg roll wrapper in half and brush with beaten egg.

3. Peel each prawn, leaving the tail on, and place it in the center of the egg roll wrapper as straight as possible.

4. Place mango and a few pieces of cilantro next to each prawn.

5. Roll each wrapper around the shrimp and place in the basket.

6. Cook in your Philips at 400 degrees for 10 minutes, shaking often.

Nutritional Info: Calories: 776, Sodium: 1370 mg, Dietary Fiber: 6.3 g, Total Fat: 5.3 g, Total Carbs: 150.4 g, Protein: 28.5 g

Quick Fried Catfish

Servings: 4 | Prep Time: 5 Minutes | Cook Time: 15 Minutes

Catfish is a southern delicacy that many may have never experienced. This recipe is a great way to experience catfish for the first time, and probably not the last after you taste it.

Ingredients:

3/4 cups Original Bisquick™ mix

1/2 cup yellow cornmeal

1 tablespoon seafood seasoning

4 catfish fillets (4 to 6 ounces each)

1/2 cup ranch dressing

Lemon wedges

Instructions:

1. In a shallow bowl mix together the Bisquick mix, cornmeal, and seafood seasoning.

2. Pat the filets dry, then brush them with ranch dressing.

3. Press the filets into the Bisquick mix on both sides until the filet is evenly coated.

4. Cook in your Philips at 360 degrees for 15 minutes, flip the filets halfway through.

5. Serve with a lemon garnish.

Nutritional Info: Calories: 372, Sodium: 532 mg, Dietary Fiber: 1.7 g, Total Fat: 16.1 g, Total Carbs: 27.0 g, Protein: 28.2 g.

Salmon Croquets

Servings: 4 | Prep Time: 10 Minutes | Cook Time: 20 Minutes

Croquet may sound like a fancy word, but it is really just a fried bread combination. That being said, your guests and family will feel pretty fancy eating these tasty concoctions.

Ingredients:

1/4 cup organic olive oil mayonnaise

4 teaspoons fresh lemon juice

2 1/2 teaspoons Dijon mustard

1/4 cup finely chopped green onions

2 tablespoons minced red bell pepper

1/2 teaspoon garlic powder

1/4 teaspoon salt

1/8 teaspoon ground red pepper

2 (6-ounce) packages skinless, boneless pink salmon

1 large egg

1 cup panko

1 tablespoon olive oil

1 tablespoon chopped fresh parsley

1 teaspoon finely chopped capers

1/2 teaspoon minced garlic

1/8 teaspoon salt

Instructions:

1. Combine 2 tablespoons mayo, 1 tablespoon lemon juice, 1 1/2 teaspoons mustard, onions, bell pepper, salt, garlic powder, and red pepper.

2. Beat egg and add to mixture.

3.   Add salmon and break apart into mixture until it is evenly divided.

4.   Mix in Panko bread crumbs.

5.   Shape mixture into 8 patties and place in basket.

6.   Cook in your Philips at 360 degrees for 20 minutes flipping half way through.

7.   Mix together oil, capers, parsley, and salt to serve as a complimentary sauce.

Nutritional Info: Calories: 335, Sodium: 595 mg, Dietary Fiber: 1.9 g, Total Fat: 14.8 g, Total Carbs: 25.1 g, Protein: 25.1 g.

Shrimp and Mango Spring Rolls

Servings: 4 | Prep Time: 10 Minutes | Cook Time: 15 Minutes

These spring rolls are a perfect appetizer for many occasions. It does not offer a high yield, but it does offer a high taste profile and are pretty easy to make for spring rolls. You will also be hard pressed to find an appetizer healthier than this one.

Ingredients:

1 pound of raw shrimp

1 cup flour

1/2 teaspoon salt

1/2 teaspoon pepper

2 tablespoons olive oil

1 mango, peeled and sliced into matchsticks

1 bunch of bibb lettuce

2 seedless cucumbers

1 avocado

1 bunch of cilantro

12 rice paper wrappers

Instructions:

1. Rinse and devein shrimp.
2. Combine flour, salt, and pepper in a bowl and sift until mixed evenly.
3. Toss shrimp in flour mix until evenly coated.
4. Cook at 360 degrees for 10 minutes, shaking often.
5. Cut mango, avocado, and cucumbers and set them on 3 separate plates.
6. Lay out each leaf of lettuce and fill with shrimp, mango, avocado, and cucumbers.
7. Sprinkle with cilantro, wrap in rice paper, and serve.

Nutritional Info: Calories: 542, Sodium: 714 mg, Dietary Fiber: 6.5 g, Total Fat: 19.8 g, Total Carbs: 58.7 g, Protein: 33.7 g.

Shrimp Wontons

Servings: 4 | Prep Time: 25 Minutes | Cook Time: 10 Minutes

These wontons are awesome because they can be used as an appetizer, side, or a main meal. They take a little more work than your average appetizer, but the results are worth it.

Ingredients:

3/4 pounds shrimp

1 scallion

1/4 teaspoon ginger

Pinch black pepper

1 tablespoon chinese cooking wine

1 teaspoon soy sauce

Pinch of salt

Wonton wrappers

Instructions:

1. Peel and devein shrimp.
2. Finely chop shrimp and scallions and put them in a mixing bowl.
3. Grate ginger over the shrimp and mix until all ingredients are even.
4. Mix in wine, soy sauce, salt, and pepper and allow to marinate for 15 minutes.
5. Roll out each of your wonton wrappers.
6. Scoop about 1/2 of shrimp mix in each one, then fold into wonton.
7. Cook in your Philips at 400 degrees for 10 minutes, shaking often.

Nutritional Info: Calories: 130, Sodium: 368 mg, Dietary Fiber: 0 g, Total Fat: 1.6 g, Total Carbs: 6.5 g, Protein: 20.3 g.

Simple Fried Pork Chops

Servings: 4 | Prep Time: 1 hour 5 Minutes | Cook Time: 14 Minutes

Sometimes simple is better, and these pork chops are an excellent example. They are not overstated, but taste great and can be paired with almost any side for a relatively quick and easy dinner.

Ingredients:

4 thick slices of pork chops

2 teaspoons iodized or sea salt

1 teaspoon ground black pepper

2 teaspoons garlic powder

Instructions:

1. Mix salt, pepper, and garlic powder in a bowl.

2. Press the pork chops into the mixture until evenly coated then set aside for 1 hour.

3. Air-fry in your Philips at 360 degrees for 14 minutes, flipping halfway through.

Nutritional Info: Calories: 262, Sodium: 1219 mg, Dietary Fiber: 0 g, Total Fat: 19.9 g, Total Carbs: 1.4 g, Protein: 18.3 g.

Spicy Southern Fried Chicken

Servings: 4 | Prep Time: 2 hours 10 Minutes | Cook Time: 15 Minutes

There are two things that define southern food—frying and spices. This recipe perfectly combines both in a main dish that is guaranteed to satisfy. This dish is nice because, while the prep time is long, it gives you plenty of time to perform other tasks in between prep.

Ingredients:

1 (3-pound) whole chicken

1 quart buttermilk

2 tablespoons hot pepper sauce

1 teaspoon cayenne pepper

3 cups all-purpose flour

1 tablespoon cayenne pepper

2 teaspoons garlic powder

1 teaspoon paprika

Salt and ground black pepper to taste

Instructions:

1. Start by cutting the chicken into pieces and discarding any unusable pieces.

2. Mix the buttermilk, pepper sauce, and 1 teaspoon cayenne pepper in a bowl.

3. Mix together the chicken and buttermilk sauce in another bowl.

4. Cover the bowl with plastic wrap and place it in the fridge for 2 hours to marinate.

5. Mix flour, the rest of the cayenne pepper, garlic powder, salt, and pepper in a bowl.

6. Remove the chicken from the buttermilk mixture and shake off any excess mix.

7. Put your flour mixture in a plastic bag then shake 3 to 4 pieces of chicken in the bag at a time until they are fully coated.

8. Cook in your Philips air fryer at 360 degrees for 15 minutes, flipping the chicken halfway through.

Nutritional Info: Calories: 1097, Sodium: 553 mg, Dietary Fiber: 3.4 g, Total Fat: 28.7 g, Total Carbs: 85.6 g, Protein: 116.7 g.

Sweet and Spicy Firecracker Chicken

Servings: 4 | Prep Time: 10 Minutes | Cook Time: 35 Minutes

This dish is for the adventurous in your household. If you can handle a little heat, the sweet will make it worth your while.

Ingredients:

1/2 cup packed light brown sugar

1/3 cup buffalo sauce

1 tablespoon apple cider vinegar

1/4 teaspoon salt

1/4 teaspoon red pepper flakes

1 pound boneless skinless chicken breast portions

1/2 cup cornstarch

2 large eggs

Instructions:

1. Start by cutting the chicken breast into 1 inch cubes.

2. In a large bowl, mix buffalo sauce, apple cider vinegar, salt, and red pepper flakes.

3. Place the cornstarch in a plastic container or bag.

4. Beat the eggs in a bowl.

5. Toss the chicken in the cornstarch, then dip it in egg.

6. Cook chicken in your Philips air fryer at 360 degrees for about 5 minutes; the chicken does not need to be fully cooked, only crisp on the outside.

7. Place the chicken in a baking pan and pour the buffalo sauce mixture over it.

8. Continue to bake at 350 degrees for 30 minutes.

Nutritional Info: Calories: 385.5, Sodium: 2720 mg, Dietary Fiber: 2.5 g, Total Fat: 6.6 g, Total Carbs: 37.7 g, Protein: 39.7 g.

Tuna Burgers

Servings: 4 | Prep Time: 1 Hour 10 Minutes | Cook Time: 14 Minutes

Tuna burgers are an excellent way to break out of the traditional burger funk. They are a healthier alternative rich in Omega 3s, and quite frankly they taste fantastic.

Ingredients:

- 2 (6-ounce) cans tuna
- 2 teaspoons Dijon mustard
- 1/2 cup white bread torn into small pieces
- 1 teaspoon lemon zest
- 1 tablespoon lemon juice
- 1 tablespoon water (or liquid from the cans of tuna)
- 2 tablespoons chopped fresh parsley
- 2 tablespoons chopped fresh chives, green onions, or shallots
- salt and freshly ground black pepper
- hot sauce to taste
- 1 raw egg
- 2 tablespoons olive oil
- 1/2 teaspoon butter

Instructions:

1. Mix tuna with mustard, bread, zest, lemon juice, water, parsley, chives, and hot sauce.

2. Stir in salt and pepper, then add egg.

3. Form 4 equal patties and place on parchment paper, transfer to fridge for 1 hour.

4. Cook at 360 degrees for 14 minutes flipping half way through.

Nutritional Info: Calories: 439, Sodium: 365 mg, Dietary Fiber: 0.0 g, Total Fat: 23.8 g, Total Carbs: 2.9 g, Protein: 50.9 g.

Tuscan Pork Chops

Servings: 4 | Prep Time: 10 Minutes | Cook Time: 20 Minutes

Pork is not a traditional Mediterranean dish, but this recipe combines the flavors of Tuscany with the other white meat. This recipe is super simple for an Italian dish and offers most of the food group staples before you even get to the side dishes.

Ingredients:

1/4 cup all-purpose flour

1 teaspoon salt

3/4 teaspoons seasoned pepper

4 (1-inch-thick) boneless pork chops

1 tablespoon olive oil

3 to 4 garlic cloves

1/3 cup balsamic vinegar

1/3 cup chicken broth

3 plum tomatoes, seeded and diced

2 tablespoons capers

Instructions:

1. Combine flour, salt, and pepper

2. Press pork chops into flour mixture on both sides until evenly covered.

3. Cook in your Philips at 360 degrees for 14 minutes, flipping half way through.

4. While the pork chops cook, warm olive oil in a medium skillet.

5. Add garlic and sauté for 1 minute; then mix in vinegar and chicken broth.

6. Add capers and tomatoes and turn to high heat.

7. Bring the sauce to a boil, stirring regularly, then add pork chops, cooking for one minute.

8. Remove from heat and cover for about 5 minutes to allow the pork to absorb some of the sauce; serve hot.

Nutritional Info: Calories: 349, Sodium: 842 mg, Dietary Fiber: 1.5 g, Total Fat: 23.8 g, Total Carbs: 12.3 g, Protein: 20.6 g.

10

Desserts

Apple Fritters

Servings: 2 | Prep Time: 10 Minutes | Cook Time: 5 Minutes

Apple fritters are a delicious and easy desert to satisfy the whole family; and this recipe even leans toward the healthier side for a desert. The hardest part of this recipe is really the timing, make sure that your fritters are shaken and removed at the just the right times.

Ingredients:

Batter:

1/4 cup whey protein	1 1/2 tablespoons greek plain yogurt
1/4 cup egg whites	1/4 cup apples
1 teaspoon baking powder	2 teaspoons soft butter

Coating:

1/2 cup erythritol	1/2-3/4 teaspoons cinnamon

Instructions:

1. Start by peeling a large apple and dicing it into small pieces.

2. Mix all of the ingredients together evenly until the batter is thick and all the ingredients are mixed evenly.

3. Place a large spoonful into your hand and flatten it between your palms; place it on a greased plate and repeat.

4. Heat your Philips air fryer to 375 degrees and cook for 5 minutes, possibly less. These cook fast so it is best to keep a close eye on them.

5. While they cook mix together the erythritol and cinnamon.

6. When they are browned rest them in the coating mix and spoon the mix over the fritters.

7. Remove the fritters from the mix and place them on a place to cool.

Nutritional Info: Calories: 271, Sodium: 75 mg, Dietary Fiber: 0.7 g, Total Fat: 4.3 g, Total Carbs: 55 g, Protein: 6.7 g.

Hoddeok

Servings: 8 | Prep Time: 30 Minutes | Cook Time: 15 Minutes

Hoddeok is a Korean fried sweet pancake that can be served as breakfast or desert. Some people serve it as the latter with ice cream. No matter how you choose to serve it, it is sure to quickly become a family favorite.

Ingredients:

Dough:

1 1/2 cups all-purpose flour	*1 tablespoon granulated sugar*
1/2 cup rice flour	*1 teaspoon sea salt*
1 tablespoon instant dry yeast	*1/4 cup milk powder*
	1/2 cup water

Filling:

1/2 cup walnuts	*1 tablespoon ground cinnamon*
1/2 cup brown sugar	
1/4 cup honey powder	

Instructions:

1. In a large mixing bowl, pour flours, yeast, sugar, salt, and milk powder.

2. Heat water until it begins to steam then combine with the dry mixture.

3. Knead the dough together with your hands and set aside, covering the bowl with a towel or plastic wrap for about 20 minutes.

4. While the dough sets combine walnuts, brown sugar, honey powder, and cinnamon.

5. Divide the dough into 8 separate pieces and roll out.

6. Make a small indent in each dough disc and fill each with equal amounts of the filling mix.

7. Fold the dough over and seal it.

8. Roll the dough into a ball and then flatten it with your hand.

9. In your Philips air fryer, cook at 360 degrees for 15 minutes.

Nutritional Info: Calories: 264, Sodium: 261 mg, Dietary Fiber: 2.2 g, Total Fat: 5.1 g, Total Carbs: 49.1 g, Protein: 7.0 g.

Fried Peaches

Servings: 4 | Prep Time: 2 Hours 10 Minutes | Cook Time: 15 Minutes

Peaches are a treat in themselves, but when you add a few extra ingredients and your air fryer they become a to-die-for desert. You will love the taste and the fact that even dressed up these peaches have fewer calories than a lot of other desert options.

Ingredients:

4 ripe peaches (1/2 a peach = 1 serving)

1 1/2 cups flour

Salt

2 egg yolks

3/4 cups cold water

1 1/2 tablespoons olive oil

2 tablespoons brandy

4 egg whites

Cinnamon/sugar mix

Instructions:

1.   Mix flour, egg yolks, and salt in a mixing bowl.

2.   Slowly mix in water, then add brandy.

3.   Set the mixture aside for 2 hours and go do something for 1 hour 45 minutes.

4.   Boil a large pot of water and cut and X at the bottom of each peach.

5.   While the water boils fill another large bowl with water and ice.

6.   Boil each peach for about a minute, then plunge it in the ice bath.

7.   Now the peels should basically fall off the peach.

8.   Beat the egg whites and mix into the batter mix.

9.   Dip each peach in the mix to coat.

10.   Cook at 360 degrees for 10 Minutes.

11. Prepare a plate with cinnamon/sugar mix, roll peaches in mix and serve.

Nutritional Info: Calories: 306, Sodium: 40 mg, Dietary Fiber: 2.7 g, Total Fat: 8.3 g, Total Carbs: 45.7 g, Protein: 10.7 g.

Fried Apple Pie

Servings: 6 | Prep Time: 35 Minutes | Cook Time: 20 Minutes

It is hard not to make a golden arches joke here. This recipe nicely replicates a famous hot apple pie and is a great specialty desert.

Ingredients:

Shell:

1 cup unbleached all-purpose flour

6 tablespoons cold butter

1/4 cup ice water

1/2 teaspoon salt

1 teaspoon sugar

Filling:

2 cups peeled apples

1/2 cup apple cider

1/4 cup sugar

1 teaspoon cinnamon

Zest and juice of 1 lemon

Pinch of salt

2 tablespoons flour

Instructions:

1. Chop apples into half inch squares.
2. Combine the flour, salt, and sugar using a mixer or food processor.
3. Cut butter into chunks and mix in, then drizzle in ice water, mix together until dough barely holds together.
4. Flour a cutting board and form 6 inch circles from the dough.
5. Wrap each circle in plastic wrap and refrigerate for half an hour.
6. While the circles refrigerate warm a pan to medium heat.

7. Add apples, cider, zest, juice, and salt; cook the mixture until it starts to bubble.

8. Cook the mixture for about 15 minutes, then stir in the flour and cook for and additional minute; set aside to cool.

9. Remove the dough circles from the fridge and roll them out until they are about double their original size.

10. Cut the new circles in half and spoon in about one third cup of filling.

11. Fold the dough over the filling and close it using the prongs of a fork.

12. Repeat this step until all of your dough and filling has been used.

13. Bake using your Philips at 320 degrees for 20 minutes, turning half way through.

Nutritional Info: Calories: 251, Sodium: 306 mg, Dietary Fiber: 1.4 g, Total Fat: 11.9 g, Total Carbs: 34.4 g, Protein: 2.7 g.

Fried Tequila Shots

Servings: 10 | Prep Time: 5 Minutes | Cook Time: 15 Minutes

Bring these to a party once and it is guaranteed that you will be at the top of the little black book every time. These shots combine everything that is good in the world and there is no way that anyone 21+ could not like them.

Ingredients:

1 pound store bought
angel food cake

1 cup tequila

1/2 cup powdered sugar

Instructions:

1. Cut cake into 1 inch by 1 inch cubes.

2. Pour tequila in a bowl and use a fork to quickly dip the cake in the tequila.

3. Cook at 360 degrees for 15 minutes, shaking regularly.

4. Pour sugar on a plate, roll bites in sugar, and serve.

Nutritional Info: Calories: 167, Sodium: 255 mg, Dietary Fiber: 0.5 g, Total Fat: 0.3 g, Total Carbs: 25.6 g, Protein: 2.0 g.

Mexican Fried Ice Cream

Servings: 1 | Prep Time: 20 Minutes | Cook Time: 1 hour

Give your fryer a break for this recipe which offers all of the benefits of the fryer without the need to use it. This delicious treat is sure to please the whole family, but may be more of a "special occasions" kind of thing due to the long prep time.

Ingredients:

5 cups cornflakes cereal

1/2 cup unsalted or salted butter

1/4 teaspoon ground cinnamon

1 (1 1/2-quart) container choice ice cream (vanilla, cinnamon, or caramel are just a few examples)

Instructions:

1. Place the cornflakes in a sealable plastic bag and crush them until you have fine crumbs.

2. Melt the butter over medium heat in a skillet and mix in corn flakes and cinnamon.

3. Pour the mixture into a bowl and refrigerate for about 15 minutes.

4. Form balls of ice cream in your hands and roll it in the corn flake mix.

5. Freeze for at least one hour before serving.

Nutritional Info: Calories: 2199, Sodium: 1977 mg, Dietary Fiber: 41.8 g, Total Fat: 120.8 g, Total Carbs: 281.5 g, Protein: 33.5 g.

Nuégados Guatemaltecos

Servings: 10 | Prep Time: 20 Minutes | Cook Time: 20 Minutes

Also known as Guatemalan orange scented dough, this is a nice sweet snack that is not over powering. Similar in texture to donut holes, they can be used as a quick breakfast for the family or when it is your turn to bring snacks to a meeting.

Ingredients:

Dough:

3 3/4 cups all-purpose flour

1 teaspoon baking powder

1/2 teaspoon salt

4 large eggs

8 large egg yolks

1/4 cup fresh orange juice

Coating:

12 cups sifted powdered sugar

2/3 cups water

2/3 cups light corn syrup

1 teaspoon vanilla extract

1/4 teaspoon orange extract

Instructions:

1. Combine flour, baking powder, and salt.
2. Make a large hole in the center of the mix and pour in eggs, egg yolks, and orange juice.
3. Mix the eggs and orange juice in the hole and then slowly mix in the flour.

4. Knead dough together then cover with a towel for 15 minutes.

5. Roll dough into 3/4-inch balls and place in basket.

6. Cook in your Philips at 320 degrees for 20 minutes.

7. While your bread cooks fill a sauce pan with 2 inches of water and heat over medium heat.

8. In a microwave safe bowl combine sugar, corn syrup, water, and vanilla extract.

9. Mix ingredients in the bowl while holding it above the water filled sauce pan.

10. Toss the bread balls in the mixture and set on parchment paper to cool.

Nutritional Info: Calories: 1202, Sodium: 150 mg, Dietary Fiber: 1.3 g, Total Fat: 5.8 g, Total Carbs: 293 g, Protein: 9.2 g.

11

Healthier Snack Options

Chilaquiles

Servings: 4 | Prep Time: 10 Minutes | Cook Time: 10 Minutes

This recipe is actually a traditional Mexican breakfast recipe, but it works great for any time of the day. It is a filling snack that is not too heavy and offers a satisfying flavor profile.

Ingredients:

12 corn tortillas

2 tablespoons olive oil

2 cups salsa

Salt to taste

1 1/2 cups shredded cooked chicken breasts or 4 scrambled eggs

Instructions:

1. Cut each tortilla into 6 slices like a pizza or pie.

2. Add olive oil to a skillet and warm on medium heat.

3. Pour salsa in the skillet and stir to thicken.

4. Mix the chicken or eggs into the salsa and simmer.

5. Brush tortillas with the remaining tablespoon of olive oil and fry using your Philips at 400 for about 5 minutes, tossing half way through.

6. Fold the tortillas into the salsa mix and return to medium heat until warm (2-3 minutes).

7. Top with your choice of garnishes and serve.

Nutritional Info: Calories: 315, Sodium: 913 mg, Dietary Fiber: 6.6 g, Total Fat: 13.6 g, Total Carbs: 40.6 g, Protein: 11.6 g.

Fried Asian Cucumber Crisps

Servings: 2 | Prep Time: 5 Minutes | Cook Time: 10 Minutes

There is so much flavor in each of these crisps you will think it is the 4th of July in your mouth. They register all over your taste buds and would be a great way to get your kids to eat vegetables or just have a healthier alternative to regular fried vegetables.

Ingredients:

1 whole asian cucumber

2 tablespoons soy sauce

1/2 cups all-purpose flour

2 teaspoons salt

2 teaspoons paprika

1 teaspoon garlic powder

1 teaspoon sugar

1/2 teaspoons fresh ground black pepper

Instructions:

1. Start by slicing your cucumber into thin slices.
2. Place the slices in a medium bowl and pour the soy sauce over them, tossing to coat.
3. In another bowl mix together the flour, salt, pepper, paprika, garlic powder, and sugar.
4. Place the cucumbers in the flour mix and toss until evenly coated.
5. Cook at 320 degrees for 10 minutes, tossing half way through.

Nutritional Info: Calories: 164, Sodium: 808 mg, Dietary Fiber: 2.8 g, Total Fat: 0.8 g, Total Carbs: 35 g, Protein: 5.8 g.

Wonder Fries

Servings: 4 | Prep Time: 15 Minutes | Cook Time: 18 Minutes

It would be pretty bold to call these wonder fries if they didn't earn the name. The potatoes themselves are pretty run of the mill, which actually gives you a chance to experiment. The real hero here is the miso sauce which really sets these fries off.

Ingredients:

1 1/2 pounds fingerling potatoes

1/4 cup mayonnaise

2 teaspoons miso paste (brown is ideal, or try chickpea or brown rice miso)

1 to 2 teaspoons fresh lemon juice

2 stalks of green onions

Instructions:

1. Start by washing and rinsing your potatoes, then placing them in a large pot covered in 2 inches of water.

2. Boil the potatoes for about 8 minutes or until they just start to soften.

3. Lay a large dish towel on the counter while the potatoes cook.

4. When the potatoes are done, strain them then place them on the dish towel to release excess water and cool down; it should take about 5 minutes.

5. Mix the miso, mayo, and lemon juice together and refrigerate.

6. Cook the potatoes for 18 minutes at 360 degrees, shaking occasionally.

7. Toss your potatoes together with the onions and top with your miso mix.

Nutritional Info: Calories: 183, Sodium: 233 mg, Dietary Fiber: 4.4 g, Total Fat: 5.3 g, Total Carbs: 31.6 g, Protein: 3.5 g.

12

Gluten-Free Recipes

Beet Burgers

Servings: 8 | Prep Time: 20 Minutes | Cook Time: 20 Minutes

Living a gluten free lifestyle is hard enough the way it is, but if you are a vegetarian on top of that it can almost impossible. These burgers are both gluten free and vegetarian, but the best part is that even the most ravenous meat lover in your family will enjoy these burgers.

Ingredients:

1-2 tablespoons olive oil

1 medium yellow onion, diced

3 minced garlic cloves

3 medium beets, peeled and then grated or shredded

1/2 cup rolled oats or walnuts

1/2 cup prunes

2 eggs

1 (15 ounce) can black beans, drained and rinsed

2 cups cooked brown rice

2 teaspoons coriander

1 teaspoon thyme

1 teaspoon salt

1/4 teaspoon cinnamon

1/8 teaspoon black pepper

Instructions:

1. Pour olive oil in a large skillet and sauté onions for 5 minutes.

2. Mix in garlic and sauté for another minute; remove from heat and set aside.

3. While the onions and garlic sauté, grate your beets and set them aside.

4. Combine prunes and oats in a food processor and pulse until mixed, but not turned into prune paste.

5. Pulse eggs into the prunes, then set that bowl aside.

6. Mash the black beans into a large mixing bowl until they are mostly mashed, it is ok to still have a few chunks here and there.

7. Pour in beats, onion mix, prune mix, coriander, rice, thyme, cinnamon, pepper, and salt.

8. Mix everything until it is combined evenly.

9. Form the mix into 8 patties and cook at 360 degrees for 20 minutes, flipping half way through.

Nutritional Info: Calories: 446, Sodium: 315 mg, Dietary Fiber: 11.5 g, Total Fat: 6.1 g, Total Carbs: 81.8 g, Protein: 17.6 g.

Crispy Enoki Mushroom and Onion Fritters

Servings: 4 | Prep Time: 10 Minutes | Cook Time: 20 Minutes

There is so much flavor bursting out of these fritters that it will be hard to have just one. That is ok though, because this vegetarian recipe is just as tasty as it is nutrient rich. Don't let the amount of ingredients scare you, this recipe is fairly quick and easy to make.

Ingredients:

2 (3 1/2-ounce) package Enoki mushrooms

1 medium onion, finely sliced

1/4 cup flour

1/4 cup cornstarch

1/2 teaspoon baking powder

1/2 teaspoon paprika

Pinch cayenne pepper

Sea salt

1 tablespoon toasted sesame seeds

1 large egg

2 tablespoons vodka or other liquor

1 tablespoon finely sliced chives

Instructions:

1. Cut the tips off of the mushrooms and break them apart into a bowl.

2. Mix onions in with the mushrooms.

3. Combine flour, corn starch, baking powder, paprika, cayenne, 1/2 teaspoon of salt, and sesame seeds, pour into mushroom and onions and mix well.

4. Beat eggs in a separate bowl and mix in vodka.

5. Pour eggs into mushroom mix and work with hands until well mixed.

6.   Scoop mix into a muffin tin and bake in your Philips at 360 degrees for 20 minutes.

7.   Sprinkle chives on top and serve.

Nutritional Info: Calories: 129, Sodium: 23 mg, Dietary Fiber: 1.8 g, Total Fat: 2.7 g, Total Carbs: 18.6 g, Protein: 4.7 g.

Fried Chickpeas

Servings: 6 | Prep Time: 12 Hours 10 Minutes | Cook Time: 15 Minutes

As long as you remember to soak your chickpeas the day before this recipe is not very time intensive. It is awesome because it is healthy, naturally gluten free, and bursting with taste.

Ingredients:

2 cups dried channa

1/4 teaspoon salt

3 tablespoons grated Parmesan

2 tablespoons chopped cilantro

1 scotch bonnet pepper

2 cloves garlic

Water to soak the peas

Instructions:

1. Pour the chickpeas in a bowl and cover in water, allow them to absorb water until they double in size, usually overnight.

2. Cook the chickpeas in your Philips air fryer at 360 degrees for about 15 minutes, shaking often.

3. While the chickpeas cook, chop up the pepper garlic, and cilantro into fine pieces.

4. Mix the vegetable together with the parmesan cheese.

5. Mix the vegetable mix with the chickpeas and serve.

Nutritional Info: Calories: 271, Sodium: 184 mg, Dietary Fiber: 11.7 g, Total Fat: 5.7 g, Total Carbs: 41.7 g, Protein: 15.5 g.

Gluten Free Fried Shrimp

Servings: 4 | Prep Time: 5 Minutes | Cook Time: 10 Minutes

Though gluten intolerance continues to gain recognition, it is still hard to find decent gluten free recipes out there. This recipe offers a delicious and healthy fried shrimp option that offers a little bit of a kick and not an ounce of wheat protein.

Ingredients:

1 pound medium to jumbo shrimp

1 egg

1 cup corn starch

2 teaspoons cayenne pepper

Instructions:

1. Start by deveining and rinsing your shrimp, then pat dry with a paper towel.

2. Beat your egg in a shallow bowl.

3. In a separate bowl, combine your corn starch and cayenne pepper until it is evenly blended.

4. Coat the shrimp in egg, then roll it in the corn starch mixture until it is fully coated.

5. Cook at 375 degrees in your Philips for 10 minutes, shaking a few times.

Nutritional Info: Calories: 293, Sodium: 292 mg, Dietary Fiber: 0.0 g, Total Fat: 3.2 g, Total Carbs: 38.3 g, Protein: 27.3 g.

Pluto Pups

Servings: 8 | Prep Time: 10 Minutes | Cook Time: 10 Minutes

It is always nice when people with a gluten intolerance can enjoy the same types of foods as everyone else. This recipe does not give up any taste or texture of a corn dog without any of the gluten.

Ingredients:

1 tablespoon oil

8 of your favorite gluten-free hot dogs

1 1/4 cups rice four, plus extra for coating hot dogs, if necessary

1/4 cup potato starch

3/4 teaspoons salt

2 teaspoons baking powder

1 egg

About 1/2 to 2/3 cup gluten-free beer

8 wooden skewers

Instructions:

1. Put oil in a skillet and fry hot dog until browned.

2. In a large bowl mix together rice flour, potato starch, salt, and baking powder.

3. Beat egg in a separate bowl, then add to flour mix.

4. Whisk in beer until you have a thick batter.

5. Dip hot dogs in mixture and place in basket.

6. Cook in your Philips at 360 degrees for 10 minutes, shaking a few times during cooking.

7. Place on plate and insert skewers to serve.

Nutritional Info: Calories: 281, Sodium: 628 mg, Dietary Fiber: 0.0 g, Total Fat: 12.8 g, Total Carbs: 32.3 g, Protein: 6.8 g.

Quinoa Cauliflower Patties

Servings: 4 | Prep Time: 40 Minutes | Cook Time: 15 Minutes

These patties are not vegan, but they are vegetarian as well as being gluten free. Though they are missing many traditional ingredients they are not missing any of the taste and these patties can be served as a main course or appetizer.

Ingredients:

1 cup quinoa

1 1/2 cups cauliflower florets

4 eggs

6 scallions, white and green parts

3/4 cups rolled oats

Sea salt and pepper

1 1/3 cups sheep's milk feta

Zest of one large or two small lemons

1/2 cup roughly chopped flat leaf parsley

Instructions:

1. Rinse the quinoa and place into a pot with 2 cups water.

2. Bring the quinoa to a boil, add salt and pepper, then simmer for 15 minutes.

3. Place cauliflower into a food processor and pulse shortly until cauliflower is broken up into tiny pieces.

4. Beat eggs in a large mixing bowl and mix in cauliflower.

5. Place scallions and oats together in food processor bowl and pulse for about 30 seconds.

6. Add scallion and oat mix to the egg bowl and mix well.

7. Mix in feta, lemon zest, and parsley and refrigerate for half an hour.

8.   Form the mixture into patties and cook at 400 degrees for 15 minutes, flipping halfway through.

Nutritional Info: Calories: 338, Sodium: 161 mg, Dietary Fiber: 6.3 g, Total Fat: 9.8 g, Total Carbs: 46.2 g, Protein: 17.6 g.

Salmon Nuggets

Servings: 4 | Prep Time: 5 Minutes | Cook Time: 15 Minutes

These nuggets are as delicious as they are healthy. There is no gluten, but there are a ton of nutrients, and a combination of flavors that may even get your kids to eat their fish.

Instructions:

2 (14 3/4-ounce) cans wild-caught Alaskan salmon

1 cup almond meal/flour

2 large eggs

1/2 teaspoon salt

1/4 teaspoon pepper

1 tablespoon lemon juice

1-2 teaspoons lemon zest

Instructions:

1. Use a fork to break apart salmon in a mixing bowl.
2. Mix the rest of the ingredients well with the salmon.
3. Form salmon into nuggets and place in the basket.
4. Cook at 360 degrees for 15 minutes, tossing a few times during cooking.

Nutritional Info: Calories: 428, Sodium: 419 mg, Dietary Fiber: 0.9 g, Total Fat: 15.7 g, Total Carbs: 24.3 g, Protein: 47.0 g.

Shrimp and Egg Pancakes

Servings: 2 | Prep Time: 10 Minutes | Cook Time: 20 Minutes

These may be more of a patty than a pancake, but it is perfect for any time of the day. These pancakes are easy to make, surprisingly tasty, and gluten free.

Ingredients:

1 pound large shrimp

1-2 tablespoons salt

4 eggs

3-4 green onions

Instructions:

1. Peel and de-vein shrimp, cut onions diagonally into 1-inch-long pieces.

2. Beat 4 eggs in a bowl.

3. Rinse shrimp and toss in salt.

4. Mix the onion, egg, and shrimp together then pour into a cupcake tin making sure that each section has an equal amount of shrimp, egg, and onion.

5. Cook at 360 degrees for 20 minutes in your Philips.

Nutritional Info: Calories: 421, Sodium: 1852 mg, Dietary Fiber: 2.0 g, Total Fat: 12.7 g, Total Carbs: 9.9 g, Protein: 64.2 g.

Skinny Carrot Fries

Servings: 2 | Prep Time: 5 Minutes | Cook Time: 15 Minutes

These skinny fries are a great little snack and a perfect way to get the kids to eat their carrots. They are incredibly simple to make and a delicious reminder that being vegan doesn't mean that you need to give up taste.

Ingredients:

1 pound carrots

1 tablespoon corn flour

1 tablespoon olive oil

1 teaspoon finely chopped tarragon

Pinch of salt

Pinch of black pepper

Instructions:

1. Cut carrots into fries.
2. Mix together corn flour and a pinch of pepper in a bowl.
3. Roll fries in corn flour mix, then transfer to a sealable container.
4. Pour in olive oil and toss.
5. Cook at 400 degrees for 15 minutes, tossing frequently.
6. Remove fries and place them back in the sealable container.
7. Sprinkle in tarragon and salt, toss, and serve.

Nutritional Info: Calories: 167, Sodium: 234 mg, Dietary Fiber: 5.9 g, Total Fat: 7.2 g, Total Carbs: 25.3 g, Protein: 2.2 g.

13

BONUS...

A cook is only as good as the ingredients that they have at their disposal. When it comes to frying there are certain ingredients that you should always have filling your pantry.

- **KOSHER OR SEA SALT** - Salt is an important seasoning in almost every recipe since the beginning of time; make sure that you have a large container of salt.
- **GROUND BLACK PEPPER** - If there is one spice that can rival salt it is black pepper. This simple spice is capable of bringing out so much flavor in a simple dish.
- **POTATOES** - You can't own a fryer and not fry potatoes. There are so many ways that you can use your fryer to turn an ordinary potato into a masterpiece.
- **FLOUR** - Flour is an important ingredient in many facets of frying. You won't be able to make bread without flour, but equally important you won't be able to bread many of your foods without it.
- **BREAD CRUMBS** - Bread crumbs come in many forms from your traditional stale bread to the increasingly popular Panko crumbs. These crumbs will keep so it is a good idea to stock multiple kinds in your pantry.
- **SUGAR** - Sugar is obviously an important part of sweet snacks and baked goods, but it can also be an important ingredient in sauces.
- **CORNMEAL** - Cornmeal has many of the same properties as flour and is often used in tandem with flour or as a replacement in gluten free recipes.
- **DRIED HERBS** - If we listed each of these individually we would be here all day. Dried herbs include oregano, parsley, rosemary, thyme, etc. They last forever and can be used to make an ordinary recipe extraordinary.

- ONIONS - Onions can literally make or break a meal; and can sometimes be the centerpiece of an appetizer. Makes sure to keep plenty on hand and a few of each color.
- OLIVE OIL - If you ever have to use oil, this is the one you want to use. It has fewer calories and healthier fats than other oils, including vegetable oil.

Next Steps...

DID YOU ENJOY THE BOOK?

IF SO, THEN LET ME KNOW BY LEAVING A REVIEW ON AMAZON! Reviews are the lifeblood of independent authors. I would appreciate even a few words and rating if that's all you have time for. Here's the link:

http://www.healthyhappyfoodie.org/p3-freebooks

IF YOU DID NOT LIKE THIS BOOK, THEN PLEASE TELL ME! Email me at feedback@HHFpress.com and let me know what you didn't like! Perhaps I can change it. In today's world a book doesn't have to be stagnant, it can improve with time and feedback from readers like you. You can impact this book, and I welcome your feedback. Help make this book better for everyone!

DO YOU LIKE FREE BOOKS?

Every month we release a new book, and we offer it to our current readers first...absolutely free! This helps us get early feedback before launching a book, and lets you stock your shelf full of interesting and valuable books for free!

Some recent titles include:

- The Complete Vegetable Spiralizer Cookbook
- My Lodge Cast Iron Skillet Cookbook
- 101 The New Crepes Cookbook

To receive this month's free book, just go to

http://www.healthyhappyfoodie.org/p3-freebooks

78310902R00102

Made in the USA
Lexington, KY
07 January 2018